MORE
THAN
NUMBERS

MORE THAN NUMBERS

DR. PAUL Y. CHO
WITH R. WHITNEY MANZANO

WORD BOOKS
PUBLISHER
WACO, TEXAS

A DIVISION OF
WORD, INCORPORATED

MORE THAN NUMBERS
Copyright © 1984 by Word Incorporated
All rights reserved. No portion of this book may be reproduced in
any form without the written permission of the publisher, with the
exception of brief excerpts in magazine reviews.

Unless otherwise indicated, Scripture quotations are from the King
James Version of the Bible. Those marked RSV are from The Revised
Standard Version of the Bible, copyright © 1946, 1952, © 1971 and
1973 by the Division of Christian Education of the National Council
of the Churches of Christ in the U.S.A. Quotations marked MLB are
from *The Modern Language Bible: The New Berkeley Version in Modern
English,* copyright © 1945, 1959, 1969 by Zondervan Publishing House.

Library of Congress Cataloging in Publication Data:

Cho, Yong-gi, 1936–
    More than numbers.

    1. Church growth.   2. Church growth—Korea.
I. Manzano, R. Whitney.   II. Title.
BV652.25.C47   1984   254'.5   83–14625
ISBN 0–8499–0366–1

Printed in the United States of America

Dedicated to my beloved
and faithful wife and co-laborer,
GRACE

Contents

Introduction

The term, church growth, is quickly becoming a popular expression throughout the world. Yet, what is church growth? Is "church growth" different from common terms already in use such as "evangelism" or "world missions"? Before I try to answer these important questions, I should give you a general overview as to how I am approaching this extremely important subject.

Being a Korean and having been saved out of the Buddhist religion, I have been able to appreciate the distinctive position of Christians who come from the Third World. We are coming from a culture which is not traditionally Christian. Korea received its first missionaries from America almost one hundred years ago. Since then, we evangelical Korean Christians have developed our own traditions. This is very important because it makes it possible for us to be Christian without being less Korean. In the past, missionaries not only brought their religion but also their culture to the countries they evangelized. So it became apparent that the new converts lost much of their natural heritage. I believe that this produced an unnecessary hindrance to the acceptance of the gospel of Jesus Christ, which is for all people. Therefore, church growth is more than just world missions, for it operates on an individual or congregational level, irrespective of nationality or cultural background.

I have already stated that I am an evangelical minister. What do I mean by that? It is difficult to label anything or anyone. However, without defining our terms we will have difficulty in communicating exactly what we mean. By evangelical I mean a basic position on both theology and life style. To put it simply, I believe in the triune God: Father, Son, and Holy Spirit. I believe that the Bible in its original text is the inspired Word of God and is the infallible final authority on faith and methodology. As an evangelical Christian, I also believe in living a morally upright life which manifests the fruit of the Holy Spirit. Finally, I believe in the reality of the new birth which causes a change of life style and brings a genuine desire to see other souls saved from sin. Although there are some differences among evangelicals concerning the gifts of the Holy Spirit as they are presently manifested, I believe that as committed Christians we should endeavor to keep the unity of the Holy Spirit in the bond of peace.

I am also writing this book from the particular perspective of a pastor who has pioneered three churches in the past twenty-six years. I have gained much by reading books which have illuminated the Word of God to me. However, not being a theological scholar, but rather having my degree in law, I must write from my own personal experience. God has been good to me. All of the churches that I pioneered are still healthy, growing assemblies. My present church now has a membership of three hundred and thirty thousand people and is still growing at the rate of ten thousand members per month.

Success has not come quickly or easily. Most of the lessons I have learned have come as a result of passing difficult tests in my life and ministry; God's grace has always been sufficient to the test at hand.

Being a pastor, I am particularly interested in those church growth principles that affect a local congregation. Therefore, I approach this book with the consciousness that not only pastors, but also sincere Christians who are concerned about their church, will be reading what I write. For this reason I have written this book in as uncomplicated a style as possible without limiting the depth of what God has taught me.

Often I read articles and manuscripts which quote my teaching on the subject of church growth. Sometimes I am disappointed with their perspective on what I am saying. Because I give a great many principles and techniques when I teach, some only hear the techniques and never catch the basic theology and spiritual philosophy which will make those techniques work. Church growth is more than a series of ideas and principles which will, when put into practice, automatically make your church grow numerically. For this reason, I will spend the early part of this book trying to state my basic spiritual philosophy as clearly as possible. I will deal particularly with the condition of a leader's heart, for this is the place where church growth must begin.

Finally, I am going to address my remarks directly to you, the reader. So often a person reads a book nonchalantly. Please do not do that with this book. I hope you will join me in the church growth journey of spiritual knowledge. I am taking it for granted that you are a committed Christian and are interested in the upbuilding not only of the church of Jesus Christ but, in particular, your own local fellowship, no matter how large or small.

Please read this book in a quiet place where you can get the most out of it. Also keep your Bible handy, as I will be quoting often from it. If you want to mark up this book, I hope you haven't borrowed it! This book is written with the belief that you will refer to it often. If you do mark it, you won't have difficulty in remembering where that portion which really helped you is located.

MORE
THAN
NUMBERS

1
Church Growth and Your Personal Resources

For many years, I have prayed for the ability to speak authoritatively on the subject of church growth. Years ago I remember praying, "Lord, I only have 50,000 members. Who will ever listen to me when I speak of church growth?" Then, when God gave me 100,000 members, I felt as if I still could not speak on the subject with any real sense of authority. A couple of years ago, I approached God in prayer again: "Lord, if You only give me 200,000 members, people will listen when I speak concerning things You have taught me on church growth." By the beginning of this year (1983), we had reached the historical milestone of one single congregation having 200,000 members. Although it is true that no other congregation has ever had a membership this large, I still feel uneasy when I speak or write on church growth. I feel that there is much yet to be learned.

In so many disciplines, research and development is an extremely important aspect of concern, but historically we have taken the development of a local church for granted. We must realize that the most important single entity on this earth is God's kingdom manifested to the world, the church of Jesus Christ. Why has there not been more studying and writing on its proper development? But as we approach the end of this age,

15

the church is again taking center stage in the consciousness of God's people.

To Grow Out You Must Grow In

The miracle of our Full Gospel Central Church is even more evident when one realizes that Korea has been traditionally a Buddhist country. As a young man, I remember praying to Buddha. I came from a religious Buddhist home. Therefore, the reality that God would raise me up to build the largest single church in the history of Christianity has to be attributable to the manifold grace of God. In the early part of my ministry one truth I learned was that to grow out, one must first grow in. By growing in I mean the development of a leader's inner resources. This is of prime importance.

I recently stopped by a building project near my home in Seoul. As I peered down at the great hole they were digging, it seemed that the hole was being dug so deep that nothing could ever fill it. Engineers as well as laborers were carefully working in the great abyss. I asked someone standing near by, "Why are they digging so deep?" The gentleman looked back at me with a smile and said, "They are going deep because they plan on building up high." A man's foundational character is not always obvious. So also a building's foundation is not obvious when the building has been erected. But when the stress of the building's purpose comes, the foundation's strength becomes most crucial. A church leader must have a strong foundation for church growth. In fact, the larger the church, the stronger his foundation must be.

Recently I was in a large American city teaching in one of our Church Growth International Conferences. A lady in her middle forties approached me. "What can I do to cause my church to grow dynamically, Dr. Cho?" she asked with great sincerity. "Lady, where is your pastor?" I asked her, looking deep into her eyes. She quickly responded, "Oh, my pastor never comes to this type of meeting." After noticing that she spoke nonchalantly concerning her pastor's lack of interest, I said, "What you can do is go back to your own church and begin to pray for your pastor. But, don't just pray for him. Begin to support his labor in the church. Once he is convinced of your sin-

cere interest in him and his church's well-being, he will come."
Church growth can never really take place without the active
leadership of the pastor. I have seen pastors send their representatives or associates to church growth conferences, but merely doing
that will not suffice. If you are a leader of a Christian group,
you must either get actively involved or find someone else to
lead. If your church is not growing, then I believe this book is
for you. If you are growing, but believe that you should be growing
at a much faster rate, then this book is what you need. Whoever
you are, I guarantee that you will never be the same again if
you carefully read on.

Changing Your Attitude

The first place that God begins the work of church growth
is in your heart. The heart is where all of our troubles begin.
Jesus said, "Let not your heart be troubled . . ." (John 14:1).
Solomon said, "Keep your heart with all diligence, for out of
it are the issues of life" (Prov. 4:23). Solomon went on to correlate
the effect of one's vision on one's heart, "My son, attend to
my words, incline thine ear unto my sayings. Let them not depart
from thine eyes, keep them in the midst of thine heart" (Prov.
4:20–22).

How does one become successful as a pastor, businessman or
in any other profession? You must first change your heart attitude.
How can you change your heart attitude? You must inspect your
vision. If you have the wrong vision or if your vision is too
small for the ability God has granted you, your heart attitude
is also going to be wrong and you will find yourself discouraged,
bewildered and depressed.

Some pastors cover up their failure by saying things that sound
spiritual. As they continue to say these things, they finally convince themselves and their congregations that not growing is
normal. A pastor once approached me after one of my lectures
and said, "Dr. Cho, I can't agree with you. I believe that God
has called us to be the chosen few." With a sigh and a pious
air, he then continued, "We don't count our people. God has
delivered us from the numbers racket." Having already heard
these things before, I was not offended at this pastor's statements.
I simply asked him to study the book of Acts, particularly 2:41,

where Luke tells us that at the first church meeting, three thousand were converted. In Peter's and John's next evangelistic meeting, we are told that five thousand were added to the church. Now if Luke thought it important enough to record the results of the first two public church meetings, then why should we ignore records that God is obviously keeping?

Being satisfied with smallness not only reveals to me a lack of insight but also a lack of compassion. With three billion people still awaiting the opportunity to reject or accept the gospel, this is no time to be self-satisfied. If there is to be church growth, God must work in the hearts of our church's leadership.

A Man's Vision Will Also Limit His Behavior

We can never be any more than we dream of being. As we set our eyes on God's holy Word and develop a deep fellowship with the Holy Spirit, our vision is changed. How can you change your vision? You can't, but the Holy Spirit can and will.

When I was first married, I took my wife for granted. I was a busy pastor and when I was not teaching, visiting, and praying, I traveled throughout the country preaching evangelistic services. I came home simply to get a change of clothing and then I would be off again. After a while my wife became depressed and would cry to me, "Why did you ever get married? You don't need a wife—all you need is a maid." I immediately rebuked her, "That is the devil speaking through you, woman." I felt righteously indignant as I continued, "I am a minister of the gospel; I am going to do God's will no matter what you say."

One day my beloved mother-in-law talked to me, "Son, I know you love my daughter. Now that you are married, you must show this love. You must learn to spend time together, get to know one another and that will also glorify God."

God took these words and used them, not only in my marriage, but also in my relationship with the Holy Spirit. I had to be delivered from the concept that the Holy Spirit was just an experience and come into the realization that the Holy Spirit was a real, divine person.

As I began to wait upon him and talk to him, he then became very real to me and began to change my vision. In fact, as we set our gaze upon the Holy Spirit, he takes the brush of faith, dips it into the ink of the Word of God and draws beautiful pictures upon the canvas of our hearts. After he gives us a new picture to strive for, we find a new internal motivation.

There is no obstacle that can discourage a man who has been given a vision by the Holy Spirit. One of the main obstacles to be overcome is the opinion of those who say, "It's impossible. It has never been done before." What is their problem? They have never seen what God has shown you. Once God has granted you a vision, then you must learn to spend time dreaming over that vision.

This is the essence of my Christian philosophy. It covers all of the principles of church growth work. I call it "visions and dreams." As I have traveled throughout the world, I have seen evidences of the fact that the application of "visions and dreams" really works in changing one's heart attitude. Several years ago, I was asked by my denomination in Australia to hold a seminar for our pastors. It seems our churches had a problem—their failure to grow. Australia is a beautiful country with strong and hard-working people. I have always admired the Australian people and had wondered how open they were to the work of the Holy Spirit.

Before the lectures began, several of the pastors told me individually about their doubts concerning the future of church growth in Australia. "This is an affluent society; Australians are more interested in sports than in the work of God," one pastor told me, looking quite discouraged. Another pastor told me, "Your principles may work in Korea, but they will not work here."

After prayer, I was sure I had diagnosed the problem. These men were satisfied with the status quo. They had congregations of thirty to fifty members and since most tithed, they could live comfortably without expanding. So often churches become exclusive little clubs. When this happens, the desire for church growth will not develop.

A humorous experience which I had upon arriving in Australia only fortified my opinion as to the church's problem. It is a long journey by air, traveling from Seoul, Korea, to Australia. When I arrived, I was quite tired. Therefore, I desired to go to a nice hotel, take a hot shower and eat a good meal. My host greeted me warmly at the airport, putting my one suitcase in his car (I always travel with very little) and drove me to my hotel. Instead of listening to our light conversation, my mind was on taking a much needed nap after my meal, then I would be ready for the first meeting. As we continued to drive, we went past the lovely Hilton Hotel, but there was a Hyatt in the distance and we were heading in that direction. To my surprise, we went past the Hyatt—in fact, we were now passing the downtown area and were heading to a poor section of town. Soon, we stopped in front of the YWCA. I was the only man in a women's hostel! Entering into the dining room was another problem. I noticed several groups of ladies looking in my direction, laughing. I went past several tables to get to the kitchen.

On the wall past the door was the only telephone in the hostel. As I looked back into the dining room, the same groups of ladies were still laughing. I felt like an Oriental animal in a Western zoo. "Please, operator, I want to call Mrs. Cho at this number, collect," I said, still feeling quite uneasy at my unusual circumstances. "Oh, darling, please give me the number of your hotel so I may call you right back," my wife answered happily. "Well, I don't know the number," I said meekly. Immediately my wife knew there was something wrong. She, with great firmness, asked, "Where are you?" "The pastors have placed me in the YWCA," I finally confessed. "Get out of there right now," she stated without hesitation.

After explaining to her that although I had the money to stay in a first class hotel, I did not want to offend my hosts, she understandingly agreed to let me stay. This incident was another indication of the larger problem with the leadership. They did not believe God for greater things.

That week I spent much time teaching the leaders to begin to expand their vision and dreams. As amazing as it sounds, it seems that our heavenly Father allows his representatives on earth to limit his activity through a lack of vision. After dealing with the question of how to expand their vision and dreams, I taught them the same church growth principles that I have included in this book. I was pleased to hear last year that since our Church Growth Conference, the Assembly of God churches in Australia have experienced a remarkable increase. After two years, their rate of growth was over 50 percent. Before our conference their growth was less than 1 percent. Since Australia's population had increased at a much higher rate, the churches there had become less significant with each passing year. Now everything was different.

What happened to the Australian pastors? Their heart attitude was changed. They had caught a fresh vision from the Holy Spirit, they had dwelt on that vision, and finally they had seen that vision come into reality. This process will become clearer to you as you continue to read.

Visions and Dreams Are the Language of the Holy Spirit

If I were to write this book in Korean, I am sure most of my readers would not understand it. If you can't understand it, this book is of no value to you. So also we must learn the language of the Holy Spirit.

Paul revealed to us an important aspect of God's language when he wrote, "God, who quickeneth the dead and calleth those things which be not as though they were" (Rom. 4:17). Paul was referring to Abraham's position of faith. In fact, Abraham is a perfect example of a man who learned how to enter into the realm of vision and dreams. Abraham was a man who was not willing to stay in the status quo. He was able to leave the known and mutually agreed upon and enter into a new place.

God's promise to Abraham was, "Go to a place that I will show you. I will make you a great nation. I will make your name great. I will make you a great blessing to all the families of the earth." If Abraham were to look upon his circumstances, he would have discounted what God had said and stayed in Haran. His wife, Sarah, was barren. He was seventy-five years old. And Canaan was a strange land. Yet, there was a basic quality in Abraham which caused him to obey in spite of every obstacle. Instead of seeing the fulfillment of God's promise, he experienced famine, forcing him to go to Egypt. In Egypt, Abraham also faced embarrassing circumstances, but he came through and returned to Canaan. Once he was separated from Lot, God spoke to him again, "Lift up your eyes, and look from the place where you are, northward and southward and eastward and westward: for all the land which you see I will give to you and your seed forever" (Gen. 13:14, 15, RSV). Abraham had to come to the place where he saw what God was promising. Before Abraham began to walk in God's promise, he had to see it. Before you enter into a new dimension of success in your life and ministry, you must have eyes to see it.

Notice that Abraham was first obedient to God in leaving the known and being willing to enter into the unknown. Although he believed God could do what he promised, Abraham had to see the promise before he could actually set foot on it. The same principle was true in the fulfillment of God's promise to him concerning a son. Abraham saw God's promise as he looked up at the stars of heaven. "Number the stars," God had said. "So shall your seed be."

God gave him a vision once Abraham had come into an obedient relationship with him. Second, Abraham dreamed of the fulfillment of that vision. He spent his evenings looking at the stars of heaven and his imagination became full of the fulfillment of God's Word to him. He would not only have a son, but his seed would be as the stars of heaven. Abraham became filled with God's promise. He would have to incubate that promise some twenty-five years before he would see it become reality, but he had begun to learn the language of the Holy Spirit, "God calls those things which are not as though they were."

Paul gives us a further description of the working of the Holy Spirit in revealing God's divine purposes to us, "Eye hath not seen, nor ear heard, neither have entered into the heart of man, the things which God hath prepared for them that love him" (1 Cor. 2:9). Paul then adds something new to what had been a general quotation from Isaiah 64:4, "But God has revealed them unto us by his Spirit." Then Paul shows us why the Holy Spirit is able to reveal God's plan to us, "For the Spirit searcheth all things, yea, the deep things of God" (1 Cor. 2:10).

We must always remember that God is more interested in our success in church growth than we are. After all, it is his church. Our problem is that our hearts have not had the proper attitude because our vision has not been correct. We have not had the proper vision because we have not entered into a deep and loving fellowship with the Holy Spirit. Now the way to deal with a sickness, I learned in medical school, is not just to treat the symptom but to get at the root cause. The sickness is a nongrowing church. The root cause is the leadership's lack of vision for the church by failure to fellowship with the Holy Spirit.

We are essentially spiritual beings, using intellect and emotion, all housed in a physical body. Our spirits are revived at the new birth, but they need nourishment and development. The Holy Spirit has been given to us as the Comforter to lead us and guide us. He has the mind of God, even for your church. Once you receive his direction and vision, you change your heart attitude from failure to success. Now you begin to be motivated by a greater force than you have ever known and you will begin to see results as you follow proper church growth principles.

Without changing your heart attitude in this manner, you can read this book and every other book on the subject of church growth and never see a change in your life and ministry. I learned this principle early in my ministry. I was pioneering a church in a non-Christian country. Just out of Bible college, I was surrounded by the poverty and disease of a country recovering from two devastating wars. All of the circumstances were negative. I learned how to fast, not because of my great spirituality, but because there was nothing to eat. These principles were not learned all at once. It took years for the Holy Spirit to develop this understanding in my life and ministry.

Right now I have a vision of 500,000 members in our local church by the year 1984. I wake up with the vision of these people filling my mind and when I go to bed they are just as real as if I were preaching to them today. At our present rate of growth and with our building program underway, I have no doubt that the vision will become reality in the time period which has been allotted.

Recently I heard the story of a couple in the automobile business in New York who have put this principle to work in their business. After just three years, they now have the largest dealership for their particular make of car in the New York City area. This is more impressive when we realize that 1982 had been a year when more dealerships had gone bankrupt in America than in any other year. God's divine principles will work in any endeavor, even in the automobile industry.

The Holy Spirit is well aware that this is the end of the age. He is now preparing the bride of Jesus Christ for the Second Coming of the Bridegroom. However, I am sobered by the fact that of the four and one half billion people alive today, over 70 percent have not been given the opportunity to accept or reject Jesus Christ. If the church awakens to the great task and begins to grow in every locality, we will see more people in heaven than in hell at the Second Coming. There can easily be thousands of churches as large or larger than our assembly on every continent of the earth.

The greatest hindrance to the fulfillment of God's desire to see his church grow is the lack of vision within the leadership of the church. "It can't happen here. This is too hard a field." These negative statements must be put out from our vocabulary, once and for all. We are to begin using the language of the Holy Spirit and building a new success consciousness in the minds of all our people.

Changing Your Self-image

"Dr. Cho, I am a no-good sinner. Why should God use me in building a large church?" a dejected pastor who was contemplating resigning his church and getting out of the ministry completely told me after a recent conference.

What is your self-image? How much do you feel you are worth? Can God use you to make a significant change in the world? (These are important questions which you should ask yourself in analyzing your self-image.)

I grew up in a country under the oppression of Japan. We lost our Korean names and language. In fact, Korean manuscripts were hidden in clay pots in the earth so that we would not lose our national heritage, which has been in existence for over five thousand years. Thousands of Koreans were dragged into Japan to serve as common laborers. Many don't realize that, when the atomic bombs were dropped on Hiroshima and Nagasaki, two industrial areas of Japan, thousands of Koreans were killed.

If anyone had told me as a child that I would be used by God to build the largest single congregation in history, I would have simply laughed. I was a devoted Buddhist and had no intention of changing. My physical condition was very poor due to a seemingly terminal case of tuberculosis. In baseball terms I had two strikes against me and a fast ball was on its way. Yet, out of this deplorable condition, God has totally changed my self-image. Because of my personal background, I have been able to understand the plight of many oppressed people who have no hope for a future. It is, therefore, my personal belief that

God can change one's self-image from one of no personal self-worth into a servant of God for whom God sent his Son to die. We are redeemed from the curse of sin not only as it affects our spirit, soul, and body, but specifically as sin affects our motivational force.

To motivate others to succeed, we must have an attitude of success not only in our speaking but also in our lives. Many churches have a nongrowth attitude because the pastor does not possess a high enough self-esteem. This is a key in leadership. The reason for a poor self-image may be one of the following: poor appearance, education, discipline, family status, ability, and health. This list is far from exhaustive but representative of the excuses given for a poor self-image.

Poor Appearance

As I travel throughout the Western world, I see a common phenomena, that is, fat preachers. Due to our Korean diet, which stresses the consumption of very small portions of fats and carbohydrates, obesity has never been one of my problems. However, I have seen so many American ministers stuffing themselves after meetings. The foods they eat are bound to cause the gaining of weight. I have heard their excuses, "Dr. Cho, I have a weight problem because of my glands." When I meet ambassadors of the world's leading nations, one of the common traits they seem to possess is general good looks. They may not be young or handsome, but they seem to be in good shape. After all, are they not representing their particular country? Should they not try to present their best image? Yet, the kingdom of God also has ambassadors. They represent the King of kings and Lord of lords.

It is my opinion that a leader can change his self-image by watching his diet and doing the best that he can with what God has given him. Take an inventory of your looks. Are you doing your best as Christ's ambassador to present an image that others should follow? If not, then it is never too late to change. Once you start feeling good about yourself, you will find others will feel better about you too. Learning how to coordinate colors and dress conservatively need not be expensive, but it will make a great difference in the way others hear what you have to say.

People will first look at you before they listen to you. What they see will affect how they hear.

Poor Education

I wish I had more formal education than I have. Growing up in very hard times limited my potential for formal education. Yet I have spent all of my life learning. People are amazed that I have an English-speaking program on television stations in America. As far as I know, I am the only foreigner on national American television. How many years did I study English in school? None. I studied books, asked many questions, and practiced. After a few years I was speaking English fluently. In most of the countries to which I travel, I speak in English and my messages are interpreted into the local language. How did I learn to speak so quickly? I had a desire, which was given to me by the Holy Spirit. I worked and practiced many long hours. And finally, I believed that I could be successful because the Holy Spirit is in me and I can do all things through Christ.

I also speak Japanese when I am in Japan. In fact, I am on national Japanese television. When I am in German-speaking countries, I practice my German. Why do I bother to learn? Because my calling is not only to Korea, but to the nations of the world. The more I know about other people's languages, history and culture, the more I am able to give them spiritual help. No person needs to spend the rest of his life uneducated. If you haven't had a great deal of formal education, then you can and should educate yourself. One of the problems I have when I travel is hearing natives of the country speak their own language in a poor manner. If the message of the gospel of Jesus Christ is important enough to speak, it is important enough to speak it well.

Poor Self-Discipline

A lack of discipline is another reason why people have a poor self-image. I have had appointments with leaders who show up one to two hours late. Traffic, business pressure and unexpected circumstances are poor excuses for tardiness. I have developed a reputation for always being early for appointments. Why? Because I believe that if someone is important enough for me to see, they are too important to be kept waiting. The fact that I can keep my appointments on time and still actively pastor the largest church in the world is due to personal discipline. Make your plans with the provision for the unexpected. If you have an appointment on the other side of town, leave a few minutes early in case of traffic. If there is no traffic, you will be early for your appointment. What a compliment to your host!

Living a life of discipline will help you to develop discipline in others with whom you work. Since I believe in delegating not only responsibility but authority, I must rely on others to help me lead my large flock. Right now, we have over three hundred full-time pastors on our staff. If I am not disciplined in my prayer life, social life, study time and business, they will not be as dependable as they need to be in accomplishing our mutual goal of building God's church.

Sin is one of the chief causes of poor self-image. It is, therefore, imperative for every person whom God wishes to use in the building of his church to live a holy life. What you watch and dwell upon will affect what you become. If there is sin in your life, confess that sin quickly to God, repenting from it and asking for his grace to live morally clean. Little successes lead to great victories and soon you will find that your self-image has changed. God is a loving and forgiving God. If he expects you to forgive your brother, why should he not forgive you?

Poor Family Status

In Korea, status is an important part of our society. Overcrowding is an historical aspect of Asian life. Confucius taught a system of ethics which is still practiced throughout most Asian countries. This culture is not known in the basically egalitarian West. People are addressed and spoken to differently, based on their status due to family, education, position or age. Yet, being in Christ, there is no difference. We might have differences on this earth, but they are temporal. Eternally, we are to be judged by our faithfulness to his calling. Therefore, I have learned to grant respect to those who deserve it on this earth, but not be limited by our earthly systems, for we are not of this world.

I don't care how low your family station is, you can change

your self-image. Remember that Jesus was born into very poor family circumstances and he is the Son of God. As you get a fresh vision of God's will for your life and ministry, you can overcome all of society's barriers and succeed.

Abilities may differ but success is for all. Our problem begins in comparing ourselves with other people. If we can't win better test scores than our friends, we give up and develop a poor self-image. The way to overcome this obstacle is to compare ourselves with the goal that God has set before us. He never leads us to do anything that he has not given us the grace and the strength to accomplish successfully. Don't judge yourself too harshly or too quickly. The scientist Einstein failed his first mathematics course. Noted millionaires have emphasized the number of times they have gone broke, but they kept on trying. Just because you have failed does not mean you are a failure. I have made many mistakes in my ministry, but that doesn't mean that I am God's mistake. I learned valuable lessons from my mistakes and I have been able to help countless numbers of people because I did learn.

Poor Health

My natural health is one of my most prized possessions. I am able to minister numerous times on Sunday, leave that night for a Church Growth International Conference somewhere in the world, and then begin ministering on Tuesday and continue all week in multiple meetings. My hosts don't usually realize how much I have done before I arrive. They believe I come to give my all to their community. I must depend on my health.

I trust God for not only healing, but I also trust him for health. Yet, I must cooperate with God in keeping my body fit. I exercise regularly and watch what I eat. I stay away from sweets. I rest as often as possible. My calling is too important for it to be hindered by poor health.

I have learned from years of not having good health. Since I was tubercular as a young man my body is not as naturally strong as others. I keep this in mind when I am tempted to take on too much work.

Stress is one of the greatest problems in keeping healthy. When I used to do everything in my church, I would collapse from exhaustion. Now I have learned to trust other people. I allow my fellow workers to make mistakes and learn from them as God does with me. I find that if I delegate, I can do much more with much less stress and energy.

However, there are church leaders who have physical handicaps. These handicaps should not affect one's ability to minister to God's people. We should take our handicaps and make them into assets. We should believe in God for healing and total restoration, but never allow anything physical to keep us from fulfilling God's calling upon our lives. Remember this, people are more conscious of our attitude toward our disability than they are of the disability itself.

The greatest disability one can have is in his own mind and attitude. We should watch the people we associate with. Are they limiting our self-image? What were our parents' attitudes toward us? Did they ever say, "You are no good. You're a failure. You're just like your mother" or "just like your father"? Often parents say things out of their own frustrations, not knowing the continuing effects their words have upon their children. Yet, by the power of the Holy Spirit, we can be set free from the disabling effects of our parents and friends. We can read the Word of God and find out what God says about us. If God did not believe we were of value, he would not have sent his only begotten Son to die for us and call us into his special group, his church. Yes, we have great value. We are able to do all that God has called us to do, by his grace.

Sometimes we pray that God would do something in our church and then we stand back to see what God does. This is a great mistake. If God is going to work in the church, he is going to work through us. If God was going to bring about church growth without using us, the church would have completed its task centuries ago and Christ would have already come. If God is going to work, he will work through you and me. This is why our personal resources are of utmost importance. What would we be like if we had the success we are believing for? The answer to that question is very important. Our character is now being prepared for the greatest explosion of church growth in history. We are being tested and we are finding grace to overcome the test. Why? Because God wants to use us.

Now we are ready to go on to the next section of this book

which deals primarily with church growth methodology. If you have read this chapter and felt that it did not apply to you, then you had better read it again. If you feel that by understanding your problem, you have overcome it, then you had better remember that understanding is only part of the solution. Yes, now you must trust the grace of God to put into practice the steps that will cause you to overcome.

As we enter into this next section, I am believing that you have changed your heart attitude. You are learning how to fellowship with the Holy Spirit, thereby receiving fresh vision and dreams. And finally, you are entering this next section with a healthy self-image.

2
Church Growth and the Laity

My book, *Successful Home Cell Groups,* was helpful to many pastors. The first portion of the book deals with my deliverance from personal ambition and fear. Both of these devastating traits will keep church leaders from seeing one of the crucial aspects of growth, that is, proper use of lay people.

Time is a limited commodity, since there are only 1440 minutes in each day. Energy is another limited commodity, since there are only so many things a man can do before his body demands rest. So how can I have 500,000 members in 1984 with these limitations affecting me as they also affect you? I have learned how to use my lay people in the work of the ministry. Right now I have over 18,000 cell leaders. These are nonpaid assistants in our church. They form the basis of my local ministry. Before I share further concerning the unqualified success of this system, there are several basic issues which need to be addressed.

What Is the Position of Lay People in Your Church?

Today, I looked in an English dictionary. Under the word layman, I was amazed at the definition: "A member of the congregation as distinguished from the clergy. A person without any

31

advanced or special skills or training," was the description of a layman which I read. I am afraid that the dictionary has put down in words the general misconception most Christians have concerning the lay person.

I find Paul's letter to the church at Ephesus to be one of the clearest and most comprehensive teachings he gives concerning the role each of us should play in the church. Paul was writing from a prison cell. His mind had contemplated long hours concerning his experience in ministry. Now without the distraction of any major alterations, he gives us in the ministry our most important task. "And he gave some, apostles; and some, prophets; and some, evangelists; and some, pastors and teachers; for the perfecting of the saints for the work of the ministry, for the edifying of the body of Christ" (Eph. 4:11, 12).

The task Paul sees of primary importance in the ministry is the *preparation* of the laity for the work of ministry. As each person enters the Body of Christ he automatically enrolls in a ministry training program.

In fact, as I read the Book of Acts, I never see God giving a new convert the option of being active. When new converts come into our assembly, they are coming with a fresh faith. It is only after they have been sitting with nothing to do that they become passive. Therefore, it is imperative that all new converts be brought into the church as active participants in the ministry. It has been my experience over these many years that with proper training, lay people become our most effective resource in evangelism.

To win someone to Christ, there has to be a bridge of trust between the person witnessing and the person witnessed to. Sometimes a person can be won to Christ by a stranger, but most often it takes a personal rapport. Every new convert has this rapport with either members of his family, friends or business associates. Every person the new convert knows is a potential new member of the church. This credibility, established over many years, should not be overlooked.

New converts also have a new-found faith which is usually glowing with the feeling of forgiveness and acceptance. Once he is trained, he can effectively convey this faith to others who knew him before his conversion. Sometimes I find new converts are quite aggressive. They may even manifest sophomoric enthusiasm. However, if you channel their energies properly, they will become effective witnesses. The apostle Paul was energetically persecuting the church following his sincere belief that this new Jewish sect was a destructive force. Once he was arrested by Christ on the road to Damascus, he zealously proclaimed Christ to the Jews and Gentiles. However, his zeal was a source of much persecution. In Acts 9, Luke tells us that the disciples sent him back to his home town of Tarsus. In verse 31, we discover something quite interesting, "Then had the churches rest throughout all of Judea and Galilee and Samaria." The churches had rest once Paul was gone. Yet, we all know how effective a witness Paul became as he was trained by the Holy Spirit.

Perhaps some of your most troublesome members are problems because they have never been recognized and challenged. A member who is apathetic is never a problem. What is the position of the laity in your church? If you view them as potential associates, able witnesses and active extensions of your ministry, your church can grow dynamically.

How Do I Train My Lay People?

There are several steps which must be followed as the new convert begins his or her training.

Step 1. Teach them how important they are to the church as a whole. In a large church, there can develop a feeling of insignificance. The larger the assembly, the less obvious each member becomes. Yet, as in a physical body, each, cell is important—so also in a spiritual body. New members must know that God has given them a gift that all of us in the church need very much. They must know that they are important.

Step 2. Motivate them. One of the most important things that a pastor can do is to motivate his people. To motivate someone else, you must be motivated yourself. This is why I spent the first section of this book dealing with personal resources. Sermons have to have a purpose. We cannot speak about topics that have no meaning to the people who are listening to us.

An American minister came to my church several years ago to speak. He began by decrying the North Vietnamese and the horrors of the Vietnam War. Although this was a topic of interest to the American Christians, it had little relevance to our Korean members. Few knew that I was adding my sermon to the one that was being preached in English as I interpreted. After the meeting, the visiting preacher was so pleased with the response he received from my members. He never knew that they had not heard his sermon. But, I believed that it was important for my people to be fed and motivated and so I took the liberty to add my message to his sermon.

Step 3. Recognize them. We give certificates to all who graduate from training. As new members see others recognized for going through a course of study faithfully, they too want to be recognized.

Step 4. Praise them. Ordinary life has little praise for the average person. All of us want someone else to think we have done something of value. This increases our sense of worth and improves our self-image. We can all find something to criticize in the people we know; but by the same token, everyone has something to praise. Positive reinforcement will work, whether it is used with waitresses in a restaurant or members in your church. If I compliment all the new members who have entered into training, I find that there are many more who desire to be trained.

Now that the new members desire to be trained, I have a program geared to meet their need. We have two Bible colleges. One is for lay people, the other is for those who are called into full-time ministry. For now I will concentrate on the Bible college which is for our lay people.

Our courses are clearly defined. Our objectives are clearly stated. Our results are clearly expected. Every new convert needs to know what and why he believes. His initial experience of conversion will not last when the winds of trial blow upon his life. He must be well grounded in the Scriptures. Yet, we must always bear in mind that this is not a pastor we are training, but this is a lay person who is being trained with the purpose of making him an effective witness of the gospel of Jesus Christ. Therefore, his training is going to be very practical. We are not going to teach him a great deal of theology. We must remember that a business person is responsible for making a living for his family in the business world. He must concentrate on his chosen field of work if he is to succeed in business. He also will not be able to relate theology to his fellow workers. He must relate Christ to them in a way which will be appreciated.

The trainee is also given practical training in evangelism. He must learn how to witness properly. Just because a new convert is motivated and sincere, does not mean that he is going to know how to witness effectively. He must also be given the biblical keys to how to lead a successful Christian life. He must learn the importance of giving. By learning how to give, he will bring the blessings of God upon his material life. "I never give to get," I heard someone tell me once. Yet, we can never be more moral than God. God tells us to give to get. In fact, he tells us that the reason we don't have is because we don't give and we don't ask. Once the new convert has completed his course of study, usually lasting two years, he is now ready to teach in a cell group.

I cannot stress enough the importance of seeing your members as an extension of your own ministry. They are the keys to increasing your hours of potential service from ten to fourteen hours per day to an innumerable amount of hours. They are the means by which you can be in many places at the same time. I have, therefore, discovered the secret of ubiquity. I am all over Korea every day through my faithfully trained members.

You are told by Paul that your main purpose in ministry is to train the saints to minister. If you do not follow the admonition of the Holy Spirit, your church will not grow to its full potential. God has not made lay ministry optional. He expects your members to be active witnesses of the gospel of Jesus Christ. The next time you speak before your people, take a good look at them. Look at their faces. Notice their eyes. Right out there, in your congregation, lies your greatest ministerial resource. Love them, feed them, but don't forget to train them.

Are you as committed to your lay people as you expect them to be committed to you?

One of the problems your members may be having is a sense of insecurity. You as a leader have been placed before them as a father figure. They must respect you and be willing to follow not only your words, but your actions. If your lay Christians sense that their church is only a stopping point on your quest for a larger or better church elsewhere, they will not have that sense of security necessary for continuous church growth. At this time, I need to ask you a very important question. Are you willing to spend the next ten years leading this particular flock?

Unless the answer is an unqualified yes, your people already know it intuitively.

You will never have dynamic church growth unless you are willing to commit your life and future to the people to whom you minister. Church growth will demand that your people follow you into a new and fresh vision. But people will not follow a plan if they feel that the plan may be changed in the future. The way to build security in the hearts of your lay people is to assure them that you are there to stay. You are willing to be obedient to the Holy Spirit should he choose to move you, but you are personally committed to them and have no desire to go elsewhere.

Later on in this book, I will present to you the keys of proper planning for church growth, but right here we need to address this important issue from a layman's perspective. There can never be more than one vision in a church. As a leader, the vision must come from you. I have already written concerning how to get a fresh vision from the Holy Spirit, but at this point I need to stress that this vision must be clearly communicated to your members. When the Holy Spirit first gave me a vision for 200,000 members by 1982, I meditated a great deal on this goal. It was not my goal, it was a goal placed before me by the Holy Spirit. But this goal came from my communion with the Holy Spirit.

Based on the goal, I laid out a five-year plan. We also budgeted our income to accomplish our goal. Then I communicated the vision, goal and plan to my people. I ministered the Word of God with the purpose of more greatly motivating my people to accomplish our goal. Therefore, my ministry on Sundays was planned with a clear purpose. My people knew where we were going, why we were going, and how we were going to get there. To accomplish this sense of direction, I have learned to preach every Sunday on a particular topic of importance that will motivate our lay people to continue to work, pray, and give toward our definite purpose and goal.

Another practice that builds confidence in the hearts of our lay people is honesty. If I make a mistake, I confess that mistake before the congregation. I never cover up an error I might have made. Telling my people the truth, whether it will hurt or not, causes them to believe what I tell them. Nothing will destroy your credibility with your people any more than exaggerating or saying something that is not so. When I first started confessing before my people, I died inside. My natural thinking told me that my people would no longer respect me and so for their sakes, I should cover up. But after many years of telling my people the truth, their love for me is stronger than ever. They no longer think I am perfect, but they think of me as honest.

As I travel all over the world and preach in large conferences and crusades, I receive a lot of money. What do I do with my money? If I wanted, I could live in a large, beautiful home with many servants, drive a big car and live like a king. My people would love me no matter how I chose to live. But my heart's desire is to give. When I feel a need in someone else, I give automatically. All the rest of the money I receive, I give to our international outreach ministry. Why do I give? Because God has placed a love for giving in my heart.

My people see my giving, although I rarely talk about it, and this serves as an example to them. In fact, it is difficult for me to write about my personal giving in this book. But I am willing to expose myself, if it will help you succeed. This does not mean that I believe in poverty. If I did not make money, I would have nothing to give to God's work. I believe that God wants us to prosper spiritually, physically, and financially. But to be blessed financially, we must learn how to give. As I give to God, God has given to me in great abundance. However, I have decided to plow back his abundance into his work. Since my wife and I enjoy living a relatively simple, yet comfortable life, we don't need a great deal of money to live on.

This attitude has produced two important results. Being the pastor of the world's largest church, I have been publicized all over the world. Reporters are always interviewing me as I travel. Not only my words, but my actions and motives are constantly under scrutiny. By living simply, yet comfortably, my personal life does not bring my motives into question.

Secondly, we have a different tax system in Korea than in most Western countries. Our church donations are not tax exempt. Our people give their tithes and cannot deduct this money from their income taxes. What would your offerings be like if you had our tax policy? Our people give because they love God. Yet, our people give because they see me set the example.

With 330,000 members in my church right now, it is impossible to touch each one of them personally. I wish I could. I love my people. I would gladly lay down my life for them. They know that to be true. But how do I show my love to our lay people? We have developed a system in my church where I can touch each one of my 330,000 members. I can visit each one of them when they have a personal need. How is this possible? The simple answer is: The Cell System.

3
Church Growth and the Cell System

"Dr. Cho, we tried the cell system in our church and it didn't work. What do you think went wrong?" an American pastor asked me recently. As I analyzed his church's experimentation with the system I have found essential in the building of my church, I discovered several problems.

Potential Problems

Although the pastor had read my last book, *Successful Home Cell Groups,* he had not participated in the cell system himself. This is a fatal mistake. Just organizing a program in your church will not insure its continued success. You must take a continual and active role in its implementation and motivation.

Second, he did not wait long enough for the truth to become an integral part of his church's consciousness. If you are starting something new in your church, you cannot expect it to take hold immediately. You first have to unteach people the wrong concepts, before they are ready to accept a new way of doing things. Most churches traditionally have viewed the work of the ministry to be the role of the pastor. You were hired to preach, visit the sick and elderly, marry and bury, and to build up the membership. Why should busy lay people do your job? Therefore, it takes months and years of teaching and motivation to change these ingrained false concepts within your church.

Third, many churches establish home cell groups by simply laying out a map of the community, picking leaders in each geographic section of that community and then saying to the leaders, "Have a meeting in your home." Even if the house group leaders obey the wishes of the pastor and start a meeting in their home, what kind of meeting does it become? Most often, the home meeting becomes simply another church service. Since most of the people in the meeting are already members of your church, why should they attend another church service?

Five Questions

The problems I have just listed are just some of the problems facing a pastor desirous of developing the cell system in his church. There are many other questions that I am sure you may be asking at this time. Therefore, I will devote this next section to answering five important questions: 1) What is a cell group? 2) How does a cell group function? 3) How do we organize a cell group? 4) How do we choose cell group leaders? 5) What happens to a cell group when it gets too large?

Incorporated in these five questions are many other questions. Although I cannot deal with every question which may be in your mind at this time, I believe that the answers to the five questions I have noted will answer most, if not all, of your questions generally.

Before I begin to answer the five questions, I want to share with you why I feel so strongly about the cell system. In Korea, we are living only thirty miles from the Communist North. The last time the Communists invaded South Korea, they were merciless on the churches and specially its leaders. When I go home from a trip through the West, I can feel the tension in the air. These godless people are just waiting to attack us. The Soviets have equipped them with the latest instruments of war, and they believe that they can unite Korea under communism. Therefore, we keep the records of all of our members in a secure place. My instructions to our staff are clear. If the Communists attack, all of the records are to be destroyed immediately.

The Communists may find us who are leaders and kill us, but they can never destroy the 18,000 cells we have developed in our church. They may destroy our large facilities, but I don't consider our buildings our church. No, the church meets every day in factories, schools, offices, homes, restaurants and club buildings. On Sunday, the church just gathers together to celebrate what God has done all week, worship our Lord together and hear the ministry of the Word of God. But the real church cannot be easily located and destroyed.

I have also noticed how some large churches develop around a strong pastor. Yet, once that pastor dies, moves, or steps down for any reason, the church empties. My church is not the church of Paul Yonggi Cho, although I am the founding pastor. My church belongs to the Lord Jesus Christ and cannot be centered on my personality. With the cell system, the actual ministry is done on the cell level. Although the people hold me in high esteem and are loyal, they can go on without me.

When I travel, I make it a point to call my wife on a regular basis. I used to be upset when she would report to me, "Yes, everything is going very well without you." Now I realize that it is a compliment to my ministry for the church to continue its fantastic growth whether I am there or not. The reality that God's program can go on without you can be devastating to your ego. This is why the first portion of this book dealt with your personal resources. As long as pride and personal ambition lie at the root of your desire for church growth, you will not be able to produce a successful cell system. As long as you feel threatened by one of your associates' success, you will be too afraid to build a proper system for unlimited growth in your church.

What Is a Cell Group?

A cell group is not a social gathering, although people do socialize in cell groups. A cell group is not a home meeting or house church, although cell groups may meet in homes. A cell group is not a center for charity, although cell groups may perform charitable acts. A cell group is not an all-night prayer meeting, although many of our cells may pray all night. A cell group is not another church service, although there may be singing, praying and speaking in most of our cell meetings. So, what is a cell group?

A cell group is the basic part of our church. It is not another church program—it *is* the program of our church. It has a limited size, usually not more than fifteen families. It has a definite goal, set by my associate ministers and myself. It has a definite plan, given to each cell in written form. It has definite leadership, trained in our school. It has a homogeneous membership, that is, the people who comprise it are similar in background.

Since you have persevered this far in this book, I am now assuming you are a church leader who is genuinely interested in church growth. I also believe that you have prayerfully considered what I have already said and you are willing to allow the Holy Spirit to make the necessary adjustments in your heart for dynamic and continuous church growth to take place in your own church. I say this because the principle details of the remaining chapters are dealing primarily with techniques. If you have just turned to this chapter and have not prayerfully read what has preceded this section, then the techniques, which I will now give, will not work in your church.

The cell system developed in my church was a slow and difficult progressive phenomenon. I wish I had been able to read a book like this, for it would have helped me avoid the mistakes which I made. Yet, through all of my mistakes, I learned that if my church was to grow way beyond the limitations of my own ability and ministry, the cell system had to become the main program of our church. For the cell system to be successful in your church it cannot be just another new thing you are trying before going on to the next new thing. Once you have settled in your heart that the cell system is God's will for you and your church, then you must be willing to invest the patience, time and resources necessary for it to grow.

In our first experimentation with the cell system, we tried to get all of the leading men, mostly our deacons, to start a meeting in their homes. As I shared in my last book, *Successful Home Cell Groups,* we found that this was not workable. First, many of these men were busy in their own businesses and sometimes got home late at night. They did not have the energy to accept another responsibility. Second, our men, being very practical and logical, felt that we had to try the system out on a small scale before committing ourselves too broadly to something that was new.

Although I could not disagree with their logic, I knew that I had heard from the Holy Spirit and must obey. If you know the story, you will remember that this new system was revealed to me at the point of great physical need in my ministry. I was exhausted from trying to do everything in my growing church. At that time our church had less than three thousand members. If God had not spoken to me so strongly at that time, I would not be alive today. This is why it is so important to hear from God as to a new and fresh vision for your church. Unless you have been given a vision from the Holy Spirit, you will not be able to persevere through all of the obstacles.

God then showed me that we should use women as cell leaders. This was totally revolutionary to us, not only as conservative, Bible-believing Christians, but as Koreans. In Korea, as in most of the Orient, leadership is a man's business. The traditional role for women was to marry, have children, and keep a good and happy home. The husband is the provider and he is in complete control of his business and home life. Although we see things changing in Korea now, our culture still is basically male-oriented. So for women to be given positions of responsibility and authority in the church was more revolutionary than establishing the cell system itself.

The first problem that I had with using women was theological. Paul did say, "Let your women keep silence in the churches" (1 Cor. 14:34). The same theme is followed in Paul's admonition to Timothy (1 Tim. 2:11, 12). However, Peter preaching at Pentecost said, "But this is that which was spoken by the prophet Joel: And it shall come to pass in the last days, saith God, I will pour out of my Spirit upon all flesh: and your sons and daughters shall prophesy, and your young men shall see visions, and your old men shall dream dreams: And on my servants and on my handmaidens I will pour out in those days of my Spirit; and they shall prophesy" (Acts 2:16–18). The promise of the Holy Spirit giving the ability to prophesy was not a promise to just men but also to women. These women had to prophesy somewhere and to someone, they could not prophesy to themselves. Paul tells the Romans concerning Phoebe, using the word translated in most places, deacon. He also tells Titus that older women should teach younger women concerning the practical responsibilities of being a Christian.

I also noticed that women were more loyal and faithful than men in the ministry of Jesus. Jesus first appeared to Mary Magdalene whose job it was to give the Good News of the resurrection to the rest of the disciples who were in hiding. As I continued to pray and study, I concluded that a woman could have a ministry as long as she was under the authority of the church. She just could not teach her own doctrine, but she could witness and minister my teaching. Therefore, I decided to use women as cell leaders in my church. Once the women began to be used and we had overcome all of the ensuing obstacles, as told in *Successful Home Cell Groups,* the men in the church became much more cooperative. In all of the years I have been teaching the cell system, I found that my female associates have been loyal and reliable. They have not rebelled and done their own thing, but have worked hard.

My advice to you then is, "Don't be afraid of using women." We have many different types of cell groups. I have found that there is a basic sociological principle which must be maintained in order for them to be successful. The principle is one of homogeneity.

My good friend, Peter Wagner, one of the leading authorities on church growth, wrote a book called *Our Kind of People.* In it, he discusses the subject of homogenous groups versus heterogeneous groups in America. By homogeneity we mean like or similar in kind. His basic theory is that churches will grow if they minister to similar groups of people. Although Dr. Wagner makes a good argument in his book, I find that we don't have the same sociological problems here in Korea as they do in America. The United States of America is quickly becoming a multiracial, multiethnic society. Immigrants have come from all over the world, bringing with them their own particular ethnic cultures.

We in Korea have had a basic cultural identity for five thousand years. Therefore, we are all Korean in race, language and cultural identity. Yet, the same basic homogeneous principle still holds true. Our national culture is divided more along the lines of education and profession. Therefore, medical doctors, college professors, and other professional people will have more in common than they would with factory workers and waiters. Housewives will find more in common with other housewives than they would with female teachers. We found that cell groups based upon this homogeneous principle were more successful than cell groups based primarily on geographical lines.

If Mr. Chun the banker is in charge of a cell meeting, his cell will be comprised mainly of financial people. Their one-hour cell meeting might take place in a local restaurant. This luncheon will look very much like a business lunch. They have a clear goal. That is the salvation of two souls per year—knowing that if they get two heads of households to accept Christ as Savior, their families will also become members of the family of God. After sharing what God has been doing in their lives and in the lives of their families, they might want to spend some time praying for their specific needs. Yet, before the hour is up, they will discuss one potential convert. Perhaps it is another financial person who is having a great problem. If that man with a need is going to respond to the gospel, it is going to be during a time when he needs more support than his family and his present religion can give him.

The potential convert is invited to the meeting. Notice two facts concerning this invitation: 1) He is invited to a nonthreatening location. Perhaps, he would never have accepted an invitation to attend my church or any other church. But a local restaurant will not cause him any fear or suspicion. 2) He is invited by people to whom he can relate. If he were invited to a heterogeneous group, he might feel totally out of place. He might wonder who these people are and whether they were on the level. But he knows at least one person at the luncheon and will be pleased to note that the others he is meeting with have something in common with him. They all speak the same language.

The men in the group will try to help the potential convert, let us call him Mr. Lee. Mr. Lee is not immediately bombarded with the gospel, but has been shown love and concern. This is the gospel in action. Not only is Mr. Chun helpful to Mr. Lee, but all of the rest of the members of the cell call him and try to be of help. Soon, Mr. Lee will be open to the message of Jesus Christ. He and his family will want to join our church, because they have already joined the family of God. Mrs. Lee will want to join one of our cells that deals with wives of the cell group. They might have joint family meetings in the homes.

But, there is a close bond developed over the years as they all feel a part of each other. Now that Mr. Lee has been accepted as a member of the cell, they can pray concerning the next person to be invited.

In the previous story, I said two men would be targeted for conversion in the year. This does not mean that more can't be reached, but that they have been given a clear goal to reach for. If they convert four men in one year, they have doubled their goal and feel very proud about it.

If the previous story sounds too mechanical to you, I must ask you, "Do you think it is important to save souls?" If the answer to that question is yes, then the cell system is for you. I have discovered that groups based on geographical considerations alone tend to bring people together who have little in common. This is what we call heterogeneous cell groups. So much time and energy will be spent trying to develop a feeling of oneness, that the main purpose of reaching the lost and caring for the sheep will not be as effective.

Yet, we must remember that the principle I have just stated is used in the developing of our cell system, not the developing of our entire church. In our church, we don't differentiate between rich and poor, high and low, or well-educated and uneducated. We are all one in the Body of Christ. But in the developing of our cell system, we try to use this natural principle for the sake of more efficiently reaching the lost for Jesus Christ.

Donald A. McGavran, who has been called the father of the modern church growth movement, states in *Understanding Church Growth*, "Men and women do like to become Christians without crossing barriers" (p. 227). This experienced scholar and missionary states many examples of the homogeneous principle working in his research throughout the world.

The clearest example of this principle can be found in the New Testament. The original church started out as a Jewish movement. Thousands of Jews accepted Jesus Christ as their Messiah. The early church met regularly in the temple and synagogues and kept the Jewish festivals. As long as becoming a Christian did not mean you were not Jewish, the church thrived within the Jewish community.

When Peter preached the gospel to the household of Cornelius, for the first time Gentiles were accepted as members of the family of Jehovah. This is why Peter was given such a difficult time and had to defend himself. After all, did not God fill these Italians with the Holy Spirit? Why should Peter deny people baptism if God had obviously chosen them?

Once Paul began to preach the gospel to the Gentile community, Jews reacted violently. Then, when Paul stated that Gentiles were not less Christian if they did not follow Jewish ritual and custom, Jews began to feel that by becoming Christians, they might not be accepted as Jews. The church then became primarily Gentile until this day. I am grateful to God for allowing the gospel to be preached outside of the Jewish community or else I would never have been accepted. But the principle remains true that people will accept the gospel if they don't feel that they must become something less than what they' already are naturally.

In Korea, I believe that we have addressed this issue within the context of the cell system. Therefore, our cell groups specialize in reaching people from different homogeneous groups, and they do so effectively.

For every thirty cells in our church, we have a licensed minister to pastor them. Our cells are also broken down into twelve districts. Each district is headed up by an ordained minister. If you ever visit our church for the English-speaking seminars we have once a year, you might want to look at our offices. Each district has maps and charts on its wall. In fact, it looks like a military strategy room. Each district leader does his work in complete earnest. This is a war we are fighting. The enemy is the Devil. The battlefield is the hearts of lost humanity. The objective is to get as many souls saved as possible before Jesus comes.

One of the problems we have in Seoul, Korea, in preaching the gospel is reaching the people who live in high-rise/high-security buildings. However, one of our female cell-group leaders conquered that problem. She took an apartment in one of the most difficult buildings to evangelize. Then she moved her ministry into the elevator. She would ride the elevator, or lift, up and down looking for ways to serve her neighbors. A lady entered the elevator with a small child and some groceries one day, so she offered to help her. Once in the apartment, our lady invited the lady to come up to her apartment and have a cup of tea.

The next day during tea, she witnessed to her about Jesus Christ. These little tea sessions continued until a few weeks later, the lady accepted Jesus Christ as her personal Savior.

Soon she had an accomplice in her elevator ministry. Now, most of the residents of that building are committed Christians. There are a number of cell meetings going on in that building every week.

In today's urban explosion, evangelism can even conquer the high-rise building. Every difficult situation is an opportunity for evangelism. Several years ago, we had a growing labor problem in Korea. Unfortunately, there was a group claiming to be a Christian organization which incited workers to rebel against their employers and strike. They targeted one of our largest confectionary companies with the secret intent to shut the business down. The owner of the corporation called me and asked if I would help him keep his company from closing down. I agreed and preached several evangelistic services during company time. Several of the strike leaders came forward and accepted Jesus Christ. They confessed their sin and had a total transformation in their lives.

Soon there was a cell meeting established during the lunch hour at the company. Many fellow workers were saved. After the cell meeting reached approximately fifty people, it divided into two cells. The results were obvious in the company's productivity in a short period of time. The owner of the company noticed that the Christians were the most productive and faithful workers, so he decided to look further into this religion. After several months, the owner of the company, a Buddhist, accepted Jesus Christ as Savior and Lord.

With 18,000 cell groups in our church, there are 18,000 stories that could be told. Yet, it is sufficient to say that once the system gets going in a church, there are no limits to growth potential.

How Does a Cell Group Function?

There is no one way a cell group takes form. It can be in a classroom during off hours; it can be in a hotel, marketplace or high-rise building. Yet, each group has a leader. The leader has gone through a prescribed training program. He is also responsible to choose an assistant group leader, so when the group gets too large the second group which is formed will have a trained leader ready to function. The cell group also has a treasurer.

Since we have learned from our mistakes, I must share with you the experience we had concerning money collected during cell meetings. Once a cell meeting has been going on for some time, there develops a family feeling within each member of the group. However, we saw a problem developing soon after the system was put into effect in our church. A cell leader began lending money to other members of the cell without any accounting being kept or without anyone's knowledge. After the problem was discovered, we realized that this might happen again, so we appointed treasurers for every group. The treasurer will give an accounting of the money received in a group and how the money has been dispersed. If there is a financial need within the cell group, money is given to the member who is in need until he can get back on his feet. However, there is a record kept of all of the financial matters and it is open for any member of that particular cell to inspect. This takes away any possibility for misunderstanding.

A cell group is not a social club. In fact, we had to limit the amount of socializing that could be done within each group. In the beginning we had families serving lovely meals when members of the group visited. However, when they were invited to another home, the hostess would try to outdo the food served in the previous home. Those who were poor felt discouraged because they could not compete with the more prosperous hosts. This situation could have destroyed the entire system, if we had not put a stop to it. Now, the cell meetings that meet in various homes during the week limit their eating to the most basic of foods—tea and possibly a few cookies.

A cell meeting must also be limited in time. In the beginning of a group, people want to drag the meeting on, some have very important questions to ask, others want special prayer for their particular problem. Yet, if the time is not limited, soon meetings will become too long and people who have to work the next day will be reluctant to attend the next session. It is also a good philosophy to have people go home when they still have a desire for more. Remember that a meal will be most remembered when you did not have too much of a good thing. In fact, this is also a good practice for your church services as well.

How Do We Choose Our Leaders?

Leadership is a quality which is inherent in the personalities of some people naturally. A good pastor will always keep his eyes open for people who naturally attract others to themselves. Sometimes people who have a natural knack for communicating with other people make excellent leaders. Most usually I find that those with leadership qualities will surface naturally. My job then is to direct that leadership quality toward useful service to the whole church.

Our leaders are not only trained in our school, but they are also motivated to use their full potential in the work of God. This is done by recognition for good service and a system of awards and certificates of accomplishment.

I cannot overstress the importance of laying out a clear goal and plan for each leader. Once a year, I personally conduct a cell leaders' convention. During that important time together, I map out what the Holy Spirit has spoken to me is the goal of each group. Recently, I had to limit the growth of our cells because our facilities were just too strained. On Sundays, the average member has to wait at least one hour in a long line just to get a place to sit down in one of our seven services.

Cell Groups Have to Concentrate on Reaching Out

I reemphasize the importance of keeping your cell groups as outreach vehicles in your church. One of the problems that a group of people have when they meet together regularly is that they become ingrown. In Korea, as in most parts of the world, the basic unit of identity is the family. A Korean philosopher once said, when comparing Western and Oriental cultures, "In the West, you have open spaces outside your homes, large lawns and gardens, but inside you have many doors and walls; in the East, we have walls outside our homes, but few walls and doors inside." The historical and sociological reality of overcrowding has caused Asians to become more contemplative in their inner beings. An Asian may be surrounded not only by his immediate family, but also parents, uncles, aunts, and cousins. This is why you see so many Oriental people traveling in groups. Koreans are no different. We are a social people. Our family relationships are very important.

When someone becomes part of a cell group, he soon develops a family tie to other members of the group. As in your family, you enjoy being together and act differently when a visitor comes into your home. It is hard to incorporate outsiders into your family unit. This is true also in the cell group. If left alone, a cell will become an extended family unit not welcoming the influx of outsiders. This is why the purpose of the cell group has to be stressed on a continual basis. Bringing in people from the outside also causes the newly trained members of the cell group the opportunity to teach someone else. Everyone has to learn by doing. If you teach someone a verse of Scripture, he will best remember that verse by immediately applying it to his daily life.

We naturally have a tendency to remember those things which we believe are most important. So also in a cell group. A new member of the group begins to be trained in the theology and methodology of soul winning. If he is not given someone to teach what he now is learning, he will not learn with the same enthusiasm as he would if he had someone to give his knowledge to. By continually having converts brought into the cell groups, we give opportunity for the newer members to encourage and teach someone newer than they are.

The Cell Group Becomes a Means of Reaching Discouraged or Disgruntled Believers

There are many people in a community who have been members of a church but are presently not attending anywhere. For some reason they join the growing number of Christian dropouts we see all over the world. Most of the Christian dropouts I have met seem to have similar stories. They still believe in Jesus Christ. They still consider themselves Christians, but they have been disappointed in the church. Some of them might have been involved in a church split. Some might have become disillusioned with the pastor or the church leadership. Some might have fallen into sin and they feel ashamed to go back to church. Some might have felt neglected by the pastor who never visited them. Whatever the reason might be, there is still a large group of people who need to be reached and touched for the Lord to heal them and bring them back into the fold.

A cell group leader is a trained soul-winner. He knows his ministry and believes that God has anointed him to be a cell group leader. However, he is also trained in counseling others. This is very important for a Christian dropout does not need to be treated like someone who never heard the gospel. Someone needs to listen to why he is wounded. I repeat, listen to why he is wounded. Then he needs to show that the grace of God is applicable to anyone who will call upon him.

Paul says that we are accepted in the beloved. We are accepted in Jesus Christ. We are not accepted because we are acceptable, but we are accepted because we are inside the love relationship between the Father and the Son. Without passing judgment and condemnation, the cell leader then introduces that wounded Christian to other members of the cell who also show a genuine concern. Once the wounded Christian dropout feels that he is loved and accepted, he is then ready to come back to church. The cell group then becomes a personal and intimate outreach to the needy Christians who are not attending any church. If someone invited them to church immediately, they might be turned off. But by inviting them into the nonthreatening atmosphere of a home or restaurant, they are much more open to express their stories. Some of the stories are very sad indeed, but all have potential happy endings.

Each cell leader knows that there is nothing too hard for God. God is able to forgive and heal every broken heart that comes to him in sincerity. The ministry of reconciliation is a ministry that can be accomplished not only by a pastor, but often even better by a layman. A cell leader, for example, may not experience the prejudice the wounded Christian feels toward pastors. The wounded person may feel all pastors are the same. But another lay person can reach him.

Therefore, not only soulwinning, but healing and bringing home those who are not attending church, is a ministry which can be effectively carried out in the cell system.

What Happens When a Cell Gets Too Large?

If you are going to have a problem, let it be due to success and not failure. We are always seeing groups which started out with just a few people, get too large for the facilities in which they are meeting, and for the purpose they were intended to fulfill. In that case the group is divided. Yet, this is not easy for some people. As a cell group has developed not only in size, but also spiritually, many of the members feel a sense of family in the group. The way to have a successful division is to keep the leadership they know. Remember, the old cell leader had been training the new leader for this purpose all along, so the new leader is not a stranger. The group will also have a successful division if the purpose for their division is continually emphasized. Cell groups are in existence to more effectively lead sinners to Jesus Christ. If the group becomes too large, then there is a natural hindrance created for people to get to know Jesus. Once people realize this important fact they will divide willingly.

Once the cell has divided into two parts, the leaders from both cells meet regularly to see how each one is doing. They keep a personal touch with each member. When one is in the hospital, that person is visited. If there is a personal need, then the leader is there. So each person is pastored far more personally than in most churches that have only a few hundred members.

After one Sunday morning service, I noticed several buses loading up with people. I walked over and spoke to the leader. "Where are you folks from?" I asked. "Oh, Pastor Cho, we are your cells from one of the suburbs of Seoul," the man answered proudly. A young man had started a cell and now there were so many that they had to rent buses on Sunday morning to get them all to church. I could never have properly ministered to the needs of that community some thirty miles away, but our cell system was there and was meeting the needs effectively.

When I teach on the cell system in church growth conferences, I usually draw a triangle on a blackboard. If you put the triangle upside down and place the pastor underneath the triangle, you are demonstrating the conventional way most churches grow. The larger the church, the more weight falls on the shoulders of the pastor. This is why so many pastors today are discouraged and ready to leave the ministry. It is not that they were not called of God to service, but they are exhausted by all of the responsibility the church has placed upon them.

However, by developing the cell system, a church can grow without destroying its leader. I show this by putting the triangle right side up. The pastor now is on top of the triangle. The size of the church does not affect the weight upon the pastor. He has come to realize that he is there primarily to train and motivate the lay people of his church to do the work of the ministry.

I am sure that you have not received all of your answers in this section. But you have the same Holy Spirit I do. The same Spirit who opened my eyes to see the reality of the cell system as God's plan to cause the growth of a new era of superchurches, can give you the specific answer you need as you go to him in an attitude of faith and prayer.

Don't be hindered by the advice of those who say, "It can't work in this community." Every town, no matter how large or small, has a key for revival. As you spend time developing an intimate fellowship with the Holy Spirit, he will give you the key to your community. God is not going to bring about church growth in your church without using you. It won't come through angels. It won't fall from the sky like rain. It must begin in your heart. It is not only for Korea. It is for every corner of the earth.

4
Church Growth and the Media

One of the chief evangelistic tools the church has at her disposal today is the mass media. Our church this year is using a considerable portion of its budget to preach the gospel on television and radio. Every day, in every part of Korea, our radio program can be heard. Once every week our church television program beams the message of the gospel of Jesus Christ all over Korea.

Media Freedom

One of the most important freedoms we enjoy in Korea is the freedom to preach the gospel over the public airwaves. Since Korea has followed the United States in many of its public policies, we have a Ministry of Communications which regulates our public media. So far the government has been fair in its attitude toward Christian television and radio. The only difference we have is that there are no purely Christian television stations. We have to remember that Korea is still not totally Christian. More than half of our population is still Buddhist. Yet, for us to have the opportunity to preach the gospel with the freedom we enjoy is a freedom for which we are very grateful to God.

We also pray constantly for the continuation of this precious liberty.

As I travel throughout the world, I have noticed that there are few countries which have the opportunity to use the public airwaves for the proclamation of the gospel of Jesus Christ. In Europe, many ministers have asked us to pray so that their governments will be able to change their public policies toward religion on television and radio. Because in America and Korea we are able to preach the gospel so freely, I believe that the church needs to use this important tool for the spreading of the gospel.

The Use of Television

Sociologists and psychologists agree that television is the main and most effective means of communication in existence today. Teachers know that what we see affects the retention of information much more than what we just hear. One way that I find I can remember something I have heard is to write it down. Once my eyes can picture it, I can remember it. In fact I read a study which stated that over 70 percent of what we know, has come through our visual senses. Truly the old saying, "A picture is worth a thousand words," is true when we analyze the effect of television on what we perceive as reality. Unfortunately, this enormous power has been in the hands of the world for many years.

Recently, I read a *Time* Magazine article stating that the rise of violence in American society was directly attributable to the rise of violence in American television. As you watch television all over the Western world, it becomes obvious how products are sold through the use of sex. Everything from clothing to toothpaste is sold through sexual connotations. Illicit sex and violence is the subliminal message that much of television is selling. Some products are sold on television through the use of pictures and words shown so quickly on the screen that you hardly realize you have seen them. These quick frames of information cause the subconscious mind to respond to products that you see on the shelf of your local grocery store. American networks charge large amounts of money for a thirty-second prime time spot on television. In fact, I recently heard that one network was able to charge one million dollars for thirty seconds during the 1982 Superbowl. If television was not the best medium of communication, then the financial and commercial world would not spend such large sums of money trying to influence people through television.

What Would Jesus Do?

It is my sincere belief that Jesus would be using television and radio to communicate the Good News. As we look at his ministry we can see clear examples of Christ using the best means available to let as many people as possible hear his words. When he spoke and a multitude of people gathered to hear him speak, Jesus moved up to the top of the hill so that more people would hear him. By the seaside, Jesus stepped into a boat and moved out on Lake Galilee so that the reflective powers of the waters would be used to increase the volume of his voice. Jesus was obviously concerned that everyone would hear him speak.

Jesus could have communicated his message of the kingdom of God in secret. He could have spoken to the disciples and then expected them to carry the message to others, but his teaching was for all who were hungry to hear the words of life. Thousands of people were able to hear him speak without a loudspeaker because Jesus knew how to position himself so that the crowds might hear.

How to Minister on Television

I have television programs in Korea, Japan, and the United States. My Korean program is different from my American program. Different societies have to be reached in different ways. We cannot expect others to adapt to us. We must study and research the audience we are going to reach before we embark on a television ministry.

When God showed me I had to come to America with television I was simply amazed. This took place when I was in Washington, D.C. speaking at the inauguration of President Reagan. Dr. Il Suk Cha, former deputy mayor of Seoul, former professor and successful businessman, told me that God had spoken to him to begin a television program in America. At first I was against it. I thought to myself, *Why should I come to the most overevangelized country in the world with television? America has many fine television ministries already. Americans will never accept an Oriental trying to teach in the English language.* All these good and proper reasons would not satisfy the Holy Spirit who witnessed in my heart that my elder and friend, Dr. Cha, had really heard from God.

I then put a big obstacle before the Holy Spirit. I said to Dr. Cha, "Elder Cha, if you are willing to volunteer your services to this ministry, I will do it." I said this with the knowledge that a successful businessman would never give up his business and high social position to work for an American television project with no pay. I was amazed again when Dr. Cha said, "Pastor, I believe that the Holy Spirit told me to sacrifice my business for his work. I will do it." Although Dr. Cha had received several degrees from American universities and had a great love for the United States, I never thought he would be willing to make the personal sacrifices a venture like this would require. Now the main obstacle I had placed before the Holy Spirit had been removed and I had a deep peace that God was leading me into American television.

I would like to use this experience of putting together a television ministry in America as the basis for sharing with you the proper eleven steps necessary to have a successful and effective television ministry.

Step #1. Know That God Has Led You

Using the television media for the gospel is not only an expensive endeavor but also a time-consuming one. If I had known the cost in advance I might not have been as obedient to the Holy Spirit. The only thing that has kept me in a television ministry is the sure knowledge that God had said to do it.

When you enter into this atmosphere, you are entering Satan's territory. He is called the prince of the power of the air. The word "air" in Greek literally means, atmosphere. The use of the airways cuts right across Satan's territory and it is going to be met with special opposition.

Step #2. Decide Who You Are Going to Speak To

This is called targeting your audience. Without a clear goal, nothing you do is going to be successful. Therefore in putting together a television ministry, you must know who you are going to reach.

Normally, my ministry on television and radio is geared to reaching the lost with the message of the gospel of Jesus Christ. However, in America, the Holy Spirit showed me that I was to reach the church with the message of church growth. He showed me that the church in America was blessed because of its willingness to give for the spreading of the gospel of Jesus Christ around the world. Yet, the churches needed someone to encourage them to pray and believe in God to grow. He also showed me that many Christians in America had given in the past so that they would see the gospel preached, but they had been disappointed with the building of large complexes which did not have relevance in the preaching of the gospel.

Prayer Mountain (see p. 99) would also be a blessing to American Christians who had sacrificed to give us our liberty and freedom through two wars. They should be prayed for. One hundred years ago American missionaries had brought Korea the gospel, now Americans would be prayed for. As I travel all over the world, I have found many who have not appreciated the sacrifices made by Christians in America and Europe. But we Korean Christians are so grateful to God for those who were willing to leave the comforts of their own homes to bring us the Good News that Jesus saves. Now the largest church in the world is not in the West, but in a former mission field. Therefore, I would ask people in America to send us their prayer requests and we would pray and fast over each letter. Yes, God made it clear that my mission in America was to the church.

Step #3. Develop a Format Which Is Natural to Your Own Ministry

It is important for a minister always to be himself. Never try to copy someone else. In the beginning of my ministry, I tried to preach like Billy Graham. I would stand like Dr. Graham, I would hold my Bible like him, and I would strain my voice to a high pitch. But I soon found out that I would tire after just a few minutes. After prayer I discovered that Billy Graham ate steak and I just ate rice and Korean kimchee. Now I speak in a manner that is much more natural to me. I raise my voice when I want to make a point, but most of the time, I just speak very naturally and always from my heart.

Since I travel a great deal speaking at Church Growth International Conferences, my television ministry naturally developed as a travel program. Every week, I bring my friends on television to a different part of the world where they can see what God is doing. Therefore, people could be blessed by seeing the world with me. Since my ministry is not only inspirational, but also educational, the format developed into an informative program. Recently, we showed the revelation of God through the Chinese language. We drew Chinese characters and explained the gospel of Jesus Christ through the characters. The cross was prophesied to the Chinese people thousands of years ago. Before the Chinese went into idolatry, the ancient fathers were aware of a unique and singular God. Based upon these illustrations we did in Singapore, I was able to spend the last ten minutes of the program teaching a helpful message from the Word of God.

Most of the people who write to me are pastors and church leaders. Many discouraged men and women write me because they know that I too am a pastor and I love them. Through the program I have received letters that have really blessed me. "My church was about to split," wrote a discouraged pastor from Southern California. "I watched your program when you spoke about receiving a new vision from the Holy Spirit, and spent many hours in prayer." As the pastor continued, tears came into my eyes. "I have a fresh anointing on my ministry now. My church is not splitting but I see growth for the first time in many years. Thank you, Dr. Cho, for being on television. I can't get to a church growth conference but I watch you every week on Channel 9 in Los Angeles on Sunday night."

Step #4. Learn to Speak to One Person

A problem that most preachers have with television is that they don't understand the medium. Television is primarily a personal medium. It reaches people, not in a public theater, but in the privacy of their own home. When you are sitting on the couch and you are relaxed in your slippers, you are not ready to be yelled at. How would you react if someone knocked on your door and walked into your living room, sat down and looked at you and began to scream? This is the way many preachers on television are viewed from the television screen. When I look into the eye of the camera lens, I think of just one person. I speak to him from my heart, just as if I were in his living room talking to him heart to heart.

Step #6. Always Be Honest

Television has a power that is different than film. It always cuts through your actions and reveals your heart. It picks up every blemish of insincerity and nervousness. If you open your heart and share what God has placed there with all sincerity, people will intuitively know it.

Step #7. Delegate the Responsibility to Someone Who Is of the Same Spirit

My director of television is of the same spirit as myself. He knows how I feel and therefore will direct the program to reflect my genuine concerns. He is an expert in the field of television— I am not. I am a preacher who has been given a charge by the Holy Spirit to communicate the gospel on television. I have learned to listen to his direction and cooperate. Sometimes I am very tired when I am doing a program. He might say, "Dr. Cho, I am sorry, but we have to do this section again. Something went wrong with the tape and I am afraid it didn't come out properly." My natural inclination is to say, "No, I'm tired, I can't do it again." But I have learned to be cooperative and do what I am asked to do if at all possible.

When I watch the finished product, I am glad I listened. So many ministers have problems because they are not willing to listen to others. They feel that they have all of the answers. So it ends up that they have to do all of the creative thinking themselves. One of the keys to my personal success in the ministry is that I have learned to delegate, not only the responsibility, but also the authority to others.

Step #8. Have a Budget

Television can sink a ministry financially. Not only is the equipment costly, but the air time is extremely expensive today. If you spend more than you believe you are able to raise, then you better know that God has spoken to you. Jesus advised that if you were going to build a tower you better count the cost. Counting the cost of something in advance will keep you from great embarrassment in the future.

Step #9. Don't Be Static

Nothing is more boring on television than keeping the same scene for a number of minutes without change. One way to see if you are doing good television is to turn off the volume on your set and just watch the picture. Ask yourself the question, "Is what I am watching still interesting?"

In the ministry we are geared toward verbal communication. We believe in the Word of God communicated by God verbally in the heart to the inspired writers. Our ministry does not normally take nonverbal communication into account. Things like body language and dress are normally not thought through carefully. Therefore, Christian television has not been geared toward visual communication.

After all, the purpose of communications is to transfer an idea from one person to another. The transference of that idea has to be understood. Through preaching a sermon in a church, you don't have a personal communication with the individual but with the crowd. You respond to the group as much as they respond to you. You can feel it when they are starting to lose interest in a particular area of your message and you can go on to something else. The crowd also has the dynamics of other people responding around them. On a platform, you move around to continue eye contact with as many of the crowd as you can. However, the same people who could sit for one hour in a church building and hear you will not usually be able to sit in their living rooms and hear you speak on television in the same way. The crowd dynamics do not function in their home. They must respond to distractions going on around them. Therefore, to communicate effectively, you must be aware of the need not only to sound interesting, but let what the viewer sees be interesting as well, without being distracting to your message. We have discovered that using other sections of video tape showing what I am talking about is most helpful to accomplish visual as well as audio communications.

Recently, I was speaking concerning my trip through Denmark. I had spoken in two church growth crusades. We chose an interesting location for me to sit in front of a restaurant where you could see the harbor in Copenhagen and the famous statue, the Little Mermaid, in the background. As I discussed what God had done in the past week, my television people showed what I was discussing. The audience just did not have to look at my lips moving, they could see what was being said.

Next year we are planning a tour of Asia Minor. I am going to do a series on the sermons of Paul. I don't only want to preach what Paul preached, but I want to go to the actual locations in which he preached his famous messages. Turkey and Greece have kept these famous spots from being spoiled. I believe that my television prayer partners are interested not only in hearing, but in seeing what Paul talked about. I believe that it will be a blessing in communicating Paul's teachings.

Step #10. Be Careful How You Raise Your Money

Money is one of the major problems in American Christian television. If you are on television to win the lost to Christ, and then your fund-raising causes you to lose your credibility, then what have you gained? I wonder as I watch American Christian television, what the unsaved person is thinking when he sees the heavy fund-raising which goes on. In Korea, we are not allowed to raise money on television. Therefore, this is not a problem in my country.

Yet I know that airtime is very expensive. In New York, we were on WOR, Channel 9, every Sunday morning. This station costs a great deal of money. However, it gave me 3400 cable outlets throughout all of the United States. We asked people to join C.G.I. to help us to stay on the air. As people were blessed by the ministry, they gave. However, we have never received one negative letter concerning fund-raising. First of all, it is not in my nature to beg for money. I would go off the air rather than beg. I also have confidence in the intelligence of the American viewing audience. I believe that as American Christians see what God is doing through the ministry of Church Growth International, they will want to participate financially.

Step #11. Don't Be Afraid of Repeating

So often we ministers think that people hear what we say the first time we say it. Most people have short retention of what is being said. I sometimes have to say something six times, before most people hear me the first time. How many times did Jesus repeat himself? He taught several basic principles concerning the kingdom of God over and over again. He used different illustrations, different circumstances, and different audiences, but taught the same basic principles. In fact, concerning the resurrection, the disciples never heard or understood his teaching until after he was dead and resurrected.

If what you have to say is important, it can stand to be repeated. I have been teaching thousands of people the truth concerning visions and dreams for many years. I still am amazed how few people understand what I am talking about. I speak concerning the fact that in praying you need to have a clear picture of what you want from God, and still many people have not heard me. I remember using the story of how the Holy Spirit taught me this lesson by giving me a bicycle, a chair and a mahogany desk. Many have told me the blessing they received from the story, but after talking to them, I realized they never got the point.

In fact, this principle is not only important for television, it is important in your preaching ministry as well.

Christian Television in Japan

We are now blanketing Kanto, Tokyo, and Kansai (Osaka) with Christian television. We tape our church program in Korea and dub it into Japanese. I use some of the same material that I use in American television, but I have changed the program because I know I am reaching a totally different culture. The results have been wonderful.

My ministry on television in Japan is mainly evangelistic. Only a small percentage of the Japanese people call themselves Christian. In fact, less than one half of one percent claim to be Christian.

It is difficult to minister the gospel in Japan. In fact, there is not a name which can be used for God. In Japan, they have thousands of gods. Therefore, just to use a proper Japanese word to signify the only one true and living God is very difficult. In Korean we have a name for God, HANNANEEM. "Hanna" is a word signifying the numerical number one. Therefore, when we say God, there is no problem in knowing that we are speaking concerning the God of the Bible. In Japan, we have no such name. The Japanese will ask me, "Which god are you talking about? The Israeli or American God, or do you talk about the Hindu gods? What do you mean by God?" Understanding their culture the way I do and being able to preach fluently in Japanese, really helps me in ministering the gospel of Jesus Christ to 120 million lost souls.

Last year a Japanese viewer showed me some pictures that had been taken the month before. The Tanaka family had accepted Christ while watching our program and had written to our office in Osaka. One of our staff members went to their home and began to study the Bible with them. They were baptized in water and joined a local congregation. Once the Word of God began to take root in their hearts, the whole family came under deep conviction concerning an image which was also a very valuable antique. What could they do with this idol? Should they sell it? How would the rest of the family react to the "insult" being contemplated by these new converts?

Through much prayer, the family decided to burn the image publicly and suffer the consequences. They took pictures of the image burning and showed them to me. Now the family feels a new freedom in their home. The rest of the family has begun to understand and Christ is giving them new-found peace.

Results of Christian Television

Many pastors go on television with a church program in order to get publicity for the church. Others feel that television will attract new members. Some even feel that a local television program will give the church credibility. All these reasons for going on television are legitimate. Yet, there are some intangible results that will justify a pastor taking his valuable time, energy and resources to go on television.

A lady wrote me a letter and mailed it to our New York City headquarters. In it, she expressed to me that she had been bedridden for many years. Through our television program she had been so blessed she just had to write me. She had seen pictures of our people praying on Prayer Mountain (see page 99). We normally have between 5,000 to 10,000 people praying day and night for their needs, revival in Korea and the rest of the world, as well as really interceding for the needs of those who write to us from America and Japan. At the close of the American television program there is a section that shows these people crying out before God holding some American prayer requests. This was not staged; it happens all of the time.

The lady who wrote to me, Sally Porter, had been so moved by the Holy Spirit that she felt led to ask God for a ministry as well. She prayed to God, "Father, You know that I am old and quite sick. I have no family and no money. Jesus, I have been waiting to die. I have been pleading with You to be able to die. Now, I want to live. If those Korean Christians can take their valuable time to work for You in prayer, I can do it to."

Her letter really touched me. I wrote her right back. In my letter I encouraged her to read the Bible at every place there was mention concerning intercession. I have since heard that she is feeling much better. She still has no family or money, but now she has a purpose in living. She goes around in her wheelchair to the other patients and gives them slips of paper on which to put their prayer requests, then she spends a full day in her room, praying for each need by name. She has been taught to be specific with her prayer requests. She is now so happy she is in the hospital, she is getting results. The other patients now come to her regularly and even the hospital staff has come to her for prayer. She now feels that she has a new family.

This was accomplished through having a regular television ministry in that community. However, she will never come to our church, she will never be a financial contributor to the ministry. But she has been transformed into a positive and gifted force in that California hospital.

Your church will benefit directly from having a television ministry in your community, which will help in your church growth. But there are people who might never respond to your appeals or attend your church who can be blessed and be made a blessing through your church program. Never go on television with the thought of just getting. Go on television with the thought of *giving* to your town something that will be a great blessing. As you start your own television ministry with this thought in mind, you will never be disappointed.

The Radio Ministry

Radio has been somewhat eclipsed as a communications medium by television. Yet, in many parts of the world, people have no television sets. The best way to reach the masses of the Third World is through the medium of radio.

We have radio programs on daily which cover all of Korea. We also have a radio ministry in Mandarin Chinese which is broadcast every Sunday to the People's Republic of China. I can't write all of what God is doing in China, but I can say this: the church in China is doing better than ever. We get reports every week as to what the Holy Spirit is doing in that part of the world. People are being saved and added to the church by the thousands. Right now, I believe there are at least twenty to thirty million Christians in China.

The way the church in China is growing is through the cell system. I can't be specific as to where and how the church is growing, but I can give you information in general. The reason for my caution is that I have already experienced saying things in public concerning the church in China and then finding out that a group was terminated by the authorities.

In a certain section of China, the cell system is working so well and so quickly, that the authorities in that part of the country don't dare try to stop what the Holy Spirit is doing. China right now is in the midst of a new thrust and modernization. In order for the new China to develop from its present economic disaster, it needs a new breed of worker—a person dedicated to the economic development of his country.

In Korea, the church grew originally because Korean Christians were perceived to be extremely patriotic. In other words, good Christians became synonymous with being a good Korean.

When the Japanese occupied our country, Korean Christians were some of the first to lead the fight for independence. The church leaders suffered great hardship and persecution. In fact, I attribute our success in large part to the blood of our martyrs who cry out for justice. They paid the price to give Christianity credibility in our nation.

So, too, in China. The Christian believers are not tied to any foreign groups. They are all committed Christians. They don't know the meaning of liberal or evangelical, but they believe everything in the Bible is true and for today. They believe in the miraculous power of God. They see miracles take place on a regular basis. But more important, they outproduce and outwork their non-Christian counterparts. They are hard-working citizens. For this reason the local authorities don't dare stand in the way of the mass conversions which are taking place in their area. To stop the evangelization of this part of China might also mean that their production quotas would not be met. So it is in their best interests to allow the church to grow.

One of the main teaching vehicles the church in that part of China is receiving is our regular radio broadcast. Since it is not coming from the West, and since I am a fellow Oriental, there is a different feeling concerning my broadcasts than their feeling toward other fine ministries also going on in Asia.

How Is Radio Different?

In radio, you only have words as vehicles of communication: therefore, you must paint word pictures. When you give an illustration, you must give many more details than you do on television. If people are going to listen and retain what you say, then you must compete with all of the visual stimuli by which the audience is surrounded. So you must give a great deal of forethought to what you say on radio.

Normally I keep my broadcasts short and to the point. I have learned that you can accomplish much more for the same price by saying what you have to say in shorter periods of time but more often. Radio is much cheaper than television which makes it more feasible for smaller churches to afford a radio ministry.

In radio you must also target your audience. You will develop an audience based on the type of ministry you are broadcasting.

If you are involved in trying to teach Christians, then you will spend a great deal of time in preparing a teaching message. If your audience is primarily the unsaved, and you are presenting an evangelistic program, then you will want to deal with important and newsworthy topics that will create interest.

It must also be remembered that radio is a more versatile medium of communication. People listen to the radio when they are driving in their automobiles, relaxing outside, and often the radio is left on when people are working around the house. Because radio does not demand the same level of attention that television does, people have a tendency to leave a radio on. This is one of the reasons more preparation is necessary in presenting the gospel on radio. I have learned that I am able to give vivid details in my messages. I also share a great many experiences on radio because human stories have the desired effect upon a person's attention level.

Why Should Pastors Use the Media?

Whether we are using television or radio, the reason these modern mediums of communication exist is for the propagation of the gospel of Jesus Christ. If you desire church growth, then you automatically desire the proliferation of evangelism. The more souls saved, the more people are going to want to be part of your church.

I believe that the pastor is the one who should be using the media. At this time the airwaves are full of evangelists who are preaching the gospel. Yet, in my opinion the evangelist needs to work with the church, not outside of it. I believe in the mass-communication ministries. However, I believe that the person who should be using the media to a greater extent than anyone else should be the pastor. He needs to have a greater burden to increase the church.

Church Growth Is a Possibility for You

You can have a greater influence in your community for the sake of the gospel. A temptation to avoid is the thought that you can get involved in doing other things on television and radio besides preaching the gospel. I am often asked about politics.

I come from a nation which to a large degree has been misunderstood by the American public. People ask me, "Dr. Cho, what do you think about your country's position on human rights?" I usually answer them, "Sir, I will tell you about Korea's position on *religious* rights."

It isn't that I am afraid of taking a political stand. I have no reason to be afraid. I just believe that as a minister of the gospel, my job is to preach the gospel. If I get embroiled in politics, I have come down from the high purpose I have been called by my Father to fulfill. Resist temptation and just preach the Word of God. If you preach the Word, people will affect their society and political situation. I have affected my community already, having 330,000 members. Politicians realize that we have a powerful voice in our country. But they also know that I am going to pray for them and support their office.

Paul asked the Romans to submit and pray for those who were in a position of authority. I could have understood this command if it had been issued to another church. But to the Roman Christians? How was it possible? Was not this the seat of the hated dictators of the world? Were not the Romans, at the time of Paul's writing of the epistle, killing Christians? However, Paul said that all authority, both religious and political, is granted by God. Jesus told Pilate that he only had the authority over crucifixion, because his Father had given it to him.

My greatest concern is with the freedom to preach the gospel to lost humanity. Not that I don't believe in social programs to help the needy. But the greatest thing you can give a human being is the purpose for which he was created. Once a person realizes that he is special, that God really loves him, he will be motivated to change his own environment. He will want to be a productive member of his society. As I refuse to get involved with political and social action groups, I come under considerable criticism from other ministers. Yet, while they are busy fighting causes, I am building the largest church in the history of Christianity.

Therefore, the use of the communications media should be used for preaching the gospel. With the use of television and radio comes a special type of power. The medium of television especially causes people to view you differently than anyone else. They all feel as if they know you personally. In a way, you are at a disadvantage. When you produce a television program, you only see the lens. When the program is viewed, millions of people see your face. They feel as if they have been with you personally, that is, if you have done a good job. This kind of power in the wrong person's hands can have a corrupting effect.

This is why Christ must deal with the motives of the heart. This is the reason I spent so much time on the subject in the beginning of this book. The personal drive to be famous and well liked by the masses, if not sanctified by the Holy Spirit, will destroy the pastor with either enormous pride, avaricious desire for money, or disastrous moral problems. The more famous you become, the greater the pressure you will come under and the more solid your Christian character has to be.

5
Church Growth and
the Kingdom of God

Several years ago, a beautiful elderly lady invited me to her home for dinner. This evening was to make a great impact on my life and ministry. Mrs. Park, a former congresswoman, joined me in the dining room and graciously sat down. As we sat before a sumptuous Korean dinner, she began to tell me her story. Although I had heard details concerning her testimony before, I considered it a privilege to hear it from her own lips.

"During the Communist North Korean attack on Seoul," she said softly. She paused as she tasted the rice that sat in front of her. "They came so quickly that most of the leading political figures did not have an opportunity to escape south. I went into my closet, found some old clothing and tried to disguise myself as an old peddler. As I was fleeing toward the South, I was arrested by the North Korean soldiers. I told them I was just a poor old woman, but they did not believe me. The soldiers took me into the headquarters building for questioning. The more I denied that I was someone of importance, the more they questioned me until one of the men took my hands and told me I was lying. 'These are not the hands of a peddler, they are too soft,' he said. Soon I was brought before one of the officers who gave me my sentence. 'You are going to be shot at dawn tomorrow,' he said very abruptly.

"The hallway was damp and cold. I could just hear the faint rumbling of traffic above me, as they took me into a basement prison cell. All I had were the few old scraps of clothes I had used in my attempt to disguise myself. By this time I was very tired and I laid down on the cement floor. As my mind raced through all of the things that had happened to me, I felt great sorrow and remorse."

What a way to see your glorious life end, I said to myself. *You have had everything. You know so many people. But tonight is your last night. What will happen to you tomorrow?* I continued to question as I fell asleep.

"It is always hard to be awakened out of a deep sleep. But when you realize that this is the last time you will ever be awakened, it is doubly hard. A young man about twenty years old took my arm and firmly led me back through the cellar hallway, up the stairs and out into the street. When the bright sunlight hit my face, I was blinded. But I was not blind enough to miss the rifle he had pressed against his right shoulder.

"We walked several blocks. I noticed the hollow shells that remained out of what were once lovely, although small homes. All of these houses were pressed against each other as if to try to protect each other from the harsh cold that had greeted us this morning. My eyes filled with tears, as I began to remember all of the major events of my life. I remembered always having to be involved. For a Korean woman to neglect marriage and the raising of children in order to lead a section of the anti-Japanese resistance—it is not common. I remembered all of the excitement as the Americans defeated the Japanese and we were all free at last. I had entered politics to pursue my goal of justice for the people. But soon I had been caught up in the social climbing that accompanies new-found power.

"My mind then went back to our little Methodist church. I sat through the sermons with disinterest, but I really enjoyed singing the hymns. In fact, I often found myself humming some of my favorite hymns when I was frightened or lonely. 'What a friend we have in Jesus,' I sang quietly under my breath. More tears welled up in my eyes and began streaming down my face as I said to myself, 'You never really ever accepted Jesus Christ as your Savior.' This statement in my mind and softly on my lips caused me to suffer even deeper feelings of pain and frustration.

"I wondered if Jesus would forgive me and save me right then? Now with all the resolve I could muster I said, 'Jesus, I am going to die in a few minutes. I have been a sinful woman. I don't deserve it, but please forgive this old woman her sins and save me like you did the thief on the cross.'

"Suddenly, I felt a joy fill my inner heart. My heart was pounding so fast, I was sure the young man, who was curiously looking at me as we walked up the hill toward the place of my execution, could hear me. I was forgiven, I was free. I was ready to die.

"I sincerely believe that no one is ready for life without Christ, but even less ready for death without the assurance that only the Lord Jesus Christ can bring. Now that I was happy and free I began to sing aloud, 'All our sins and griefs to bear, what a privilege to carry, everything to God in prayer.'

" 'Shut up, old woman!' the boy turned soldier shouted at me. 'Stop your singing now!'

" 'Why should I obey you now?' I asked. 'Isn't it true that I am going to die anyway? I am now a Christian, I was just saved walking up this hill and I will take my last few minutes left on this earth to praise my Lord and Savior, Jesus Christ.'

" 'Blessed assurance, Jesus is mine; oh, what a fortaste of glory divine.' I started a new hymn just for the rude young soldier. Suddenly, all of the words of this hymn came back into my memory and I continued to sing as loud as I could. At the side of another hill on the outskirts of the city, I noticed there was a flat area. The young man took out a shovel and began to dig my grave. As he dug, I continued singing. He occasionally looked up at me, then would continue digging. When he was finished, he took a blindfold, put it over my eyes and said, 'Old woman, do you have any last words you want to say before I kill you and bury your body?' Although my eyes were blindfolded, I felt I could see right into the heart of the young executioner in front of me.

" 'Yes,' I said feeling sorry for him, 'I have only a few things to say. I have led a very wonderful life on this earth. But as we walked up here you had to notice that something happened to me. I woke up this morning full of fear. Now I have peace and joy. You see, I was only a nominal Christian this morning, but now I am saved. I only wish you too could know this wonderful Savior Jesus Christ.' I could have said more, but right at that moment I felt someone telling me to pray for my young guard.

" 'May I spend the last moments of my life praying for your soul?' I asked, stepping down into the hole that he had dug which was to be my grave. I knelt down and began to pray. After only praying a few minutes, I heard the young man crying. I finished my prayer and said, 'I am finished. You may shoot me now.' But nothing happened. What could be wrong? I said, 'I am finished praying. You may shoot.'

" 'I can't,' I heard him say above what I perceived to be sobs of agonizing tears. He stepped down into the grave, pulled off my blindfold and looked me in the eyes. 'My mother used to pray for me like that. I can see her praying for me now. When I lifted up my rifle to shoot you, I saw a vision of my mother and I can't shoot my mother.'

" 'You must obey your orders or they will kill you,' I said, now concerned more for his life than I was for my own.

" 'I can't kill you. Please, run away when I shoot into the sky,' he said, as he untied my hands, and let me go. I ran into the hills to safety."

By the time Mrs. Park had finished the story, I found myself crying with her, not concerned that I had hardly eaten the food. Mrs. Park is now in heaven, but she spent the rest of her life witnessing to leaders concerning Jesus Christ's ability to deliver and set prisoners free. She started the first presidential prayer breakfast in Korea and was able to touch the hearts of many of our most powerful political and economic leaders. However, I remember her looking me in the eye at the end of her story and saying something to me that has had a great impact.

"Pastor Cho, you are a young man. You have a great future in the ministry. But I have to advise you about something which you are never to forget. Preach the kingdom of God. Never get sidetracked. Preach all of the gospel of the kingdom. Never allow convenience or prominence to keep you from preaching the message that Jesus preached. Again I say, preach the kingdom of God!"

I have never forgotten these words from this Korean saint.

Therefore, I will share the importance of preaching the kingdom of God and seeing the power of the kingdom of God in action.

What Is the Gospel of the Kingdom of God?

Before we know what Jesus meant by the gospel of the kingdom, we have to try to understand what the kingdom of God is. The kingdom of God is twofold. There is the future aspect of the kingdom of God and there is the present reality of the kingdom of God. Although there are many facets of this important biblical topic, I think that it is important to every Christian to understand how the kingdom of God affects church growth. Once we understand this important lesson, we can release dynamic power that lies within every believer. We can see the power of the Holy Spirit at work in our ministry as the first apostles experienced.

What Is the Kingdom of God?

Since the beginning of recorded human experience, men have always tried to fathom an ideal society. Plato, the well-known Greek philosopher, dreamed of an ideal society based upon an ethical political framework. His republic became a model for future societies to contemplate, but Plato himself realized that his political and social philosophies were too idealistic ever to be executed to his desired perfection.

The Old Testament prophets spoke of a future age when men would live together without armaments of war. Isaiah spoke of spears being turned into pruning hooks, and nations not lifting up swords against each other. In fact, the peace of the world would be so dramatically different that he used the images of a wolf lying down with a lamb, leopards with kids, and calves with young lions to signify the radical change in world affairs which would come in the future.

The message which Jesus preached was one of repentance because the beginning of a new era was at hand. "Repent, for the kingdom of heaven is at hand" (Matt. 4:17). His teachings, illustrations, and parables were all primarily dealing with the kingdom of God. In fact the prayer he taught the disciples to pray was, "Thy kingdom come, thy will be done on earth as it is in heaven" (Matt. 6:10).

To the very end, Jesus continually emphasized the kingdom to his disciples. Although it is obvious to all who study the gospels that Jesus' main emphasis was on the kingdom of God (Matthew called it the kingdom of heaven because he wrote primarily for the Jews), I find little agreement on what the kingdom of God is and what the message of the gospel of the kingdom should be.

Augustine perceived the kingdom of God to be synonymous with the church. The Reformed movement had a large part in redefining the meaning of the kingdom of God. Calvin basically agreed with Augustine. He differed on what aspect of the church represented the kingdom of God. His feelings were that the true church which was within the obvious church was the earthly manifestation of the kingdom of God. It has the task of changing the nations of this world into people willing to submit to the lordship of Jesus Christ. The task of the church would be made possible by the use of a special power called the gospel of the kingdom of God. This gospel of the kingdom of God would so affect the lives of first men and then nations that there would be a mighty transformation of social, political, and economic reality. The church was likened to leaven which would slowly so permeate the dough of the earth that at a point in history the earth would proclaim Jesus Christ as Lord and King. At this point the Lord Jesus Christ would return to earth to accept the kingdom prepared for him by his heavenly Father.

There has been another school of theology which does not try to explain the kingdom of God in terms of the future but tries to understand the kingdom of God in its present social context. Harvey Cox is just one of many modern theologians who view the kingdom of God as a social order brought about by the church. The problems of inequality, prejudice, as well as the rest of our social concerns are to be addressed and dealt with by a church which is conscious of its mission. Biblical terms are redefined to make them more relevant to today's problems. Many of our liberal church leaders are motivated by what they see is the lack of concern within the more conservative evangelical church leaders.

Although my view of the kingdom of God will be dealt with later in this chapter, I believe that there is a basic flaw in just a theological view of the kingdom of God. Although I believe in reason, I don't believe in reason's infallibility. There is a greater foundation than reason in establishing what the kingdom of God really is. That foundation is the simple and yet profound Word of God. Let us look at some basic biblical principles which will help us understand what the kingdom of God is.

1. The kingdom of God is not only for the future, but also for the present. "For the kingdom of God is not meat and drink; but righteousness, and peace, and joy in the Holy Ghost" (Rom. 14:17). Paul reveals to us that the kingdom of God transcends the natural existence of man and causes him to experience in the here and now, the fruit of the Holy Spirit. That if you associate with the Holy Spirit you will become like the person you are associating with. The natural result of association with the Holy Spirit will be a way of life which is more concerned with the quality God bestows to life rather than the essential aspects to life, eating and drinking.

2. Paul also reveals that the kingdom of God is something that we have entered into as a result of our being regenerated by the Holy Spirit. "[God] hath delivered us from the power of darkness, and hath translated us into the kingdom of his dear Son" (Col. 1:13).

The word, "translated," used in our English text, in the Greek is *metestasen* which literally means to change sides.

As I study this verse, I see a picture of a football game. Each team is on the opposite end of the field. On one side is the team which represents the kingdom of darkness. On the other side is the team which represents the kingdom of God. During the game, one of the main players of the darkness team takes off his shirt and number, goes to the opposing bench and puts on the kingdom of God shirt. Then he goes on the field to play against the darkness boys. He simply switches sides.

This is what happened to us. We were transformed from one kingdom to the other, the kingdom of our Lord.

3. The kingdom of God is also described in its future prospect for eternal blessedness: "Wherefore the rather, brethren, give diligence to make your calling and election sure: for if ye do these things, ye shall never fall: For so an entrance shall be ministered unto you abundantly in the everlasting kingdom of our Lord and Saviour Jesus Christ" (2 Peter 1:10, 11).

In Matthew Jesus spoke of the future when he said, "Many

will come from the east and west and sit at the table with Abraham, Isaac and Jacob in the kingdom of heaven" (8:11).

Yet in Matthew 13, our Lord tells parables which give further clarification to what he meant by the kingdom of heaven. He says that once the kingdom is purged, the righteous would shine like the sun.

4. Jesus is the representation of what it is like to be in the kingdom. "The kingdom of God is not coming with signs to be observed; nor will they say, 'Lo, here it is!' or 'There!' for behold, the kingdom of God is in the midst of you" (Luke 17:20–21, RSV).

This verse can be applied to the fact that the kingdom of God was there in their midst. The "you" here is the plural, which in English is hard to understand. Jesus was there in their midst. The Pharisees were not to look for a glorious manifestation in the future, but the kingdom was before them and they were too blind to observe that God was working without a lot of fanfare.

5. The kingdom's paradox has to be viewed on the basis of a balanced understanding. Jesus told Pilate in John 18, "My kingdom is not of this world." Yet he also said in Luke 13 that the kingdom of God would start out rather unobservably, like a mustard seed. Yet, this seed, almost unnoticed, would grow up and affect the entire world.

Rather than seeing opposing views in Scripture as contradictory, I consider them as a balance. Therefore, the kingdom of God is future, but it is present. It is not of this world, but it affects this world. It can be entered into at the present time, but there is a future fulfillment.

You can't see it with the natural eye, but the kingdom of God is everywhere Christ is. As we analyze the kingdom further we realize that the word kingdom can be understood in different ways.

Both the word *baileia,* the Greek word translated kingdom; and the Hebrew word *malkuth* signify the rank and authority exercised by a king. Our present thinking deals with the people who are under the king's authority or the actual territory over which kingly authority is exercised. So the nature of the authority may be closer to the understanding of the biblical concept of kingdom than the actual subjects of the authority.

Psalm 145:13 expresses in poetic terms something of this idea, "Thy kingdom is an everlasting kingdom, and thy dominion endureth throughout all generations." In classical Hebrew poetry, the two verses of the poem are to express the same idea in differing ways. Therefore the poet's concept of the kingdom was that it was God's actual dominion.

Herod the Great was not a popular king of Israel. Although he rebuilt the temple to majestic grandeur and built a great many fine public buildings in Jerusalem, he had no real kingdom. There was no genuine basis for his authority apart from Roman might. He had gone to Rome and had been given the kingship over Israel without a legitimate basis for having this kind of authority. He was not born to it. He was not anointed by a recognized prophet. He was not a descendant of Judah. He had no legitimacy. Although he lived in a palace, wore a crown and was called King Herod, his kingdom was bought and not earned. In Great Britain there are estates that can be bought which will carry a title with them. So if you have enough money, you may buy a title. Yet, this is not the same as being given a title by the queen. Or being born into a noble family. Money might buy you a title, but that title is not legitimate.

As we analyze this thinking further, it causes us to understand the prayer which Jesus told us to pray: "Thy kingdom come. Thy will be done in earth, as it is in heaven." More than asking God to take over the world in a cataclysmic event, there seems to be desire in the heart of the Lord for the authority of God to be as obvious to the earth as it is obvious in heaven.

Therefore I believe that the kingdom of God is the nature of his reign or his authority. It is genuine, it is undisputable, and it is eternal. The reign of God is present, but it will also be in the future. God has always been in charge! He is the Creator of the earth and for that matter the entire universe. He is all powerful. However, in this human arena called earth, God has allowed himself to be limited. Satan was given a realm of authority. He is the god of this present age. He has authority over this world's systems. His seat of authority is in the immediate atmosphere surrounding the world. But God has not allowed for man to be at his mercy. He has provided an escape from the territory over which Satan has authority. He provided Jesus Christ, the last Adam.

The last Adam has given all those who trust him, all that the original Adam lost and more. For now man is included inside a love relationship. He is accepted in the beloved.

Yet, Christ came into Satan's territory and had to earn the right to stake out the territory for the opposing side, the kingdom of light. God does not break his divine word. For Satan's authority to be diminished, he would have to forfeit that authority. Satan therefore had to try to destroy the child. But God protected him. Satan tempted the man, Jesus Christ, but Christ won the contest. As soon as Satan lost round one of the contest for the authority to rule this earth, Jesus manifested the power of the kingdom of God. He healed the sick and cast out demons.

Jesus called disciples who were not only given his power and sent, but they were also tested. The seventy were sent out to heal the sick and cast out demons. They were amazed that they also had authority.

Satan's last contest with Christ came at the cross. Satan, through the entire realm or authority granted him, had fixed the odds. He would kill the Son of God and scatter the disciples. No longer would he have to fear contradiction to the right of his rule. Jesus not only died but on the third day, he rose from the dead and conquered Satan and all of his forces. He took the keys of death and Hades itself and was proclaimed Lord of all.

Before Jesus rose from the earth and ascended back to his Father, he said, "All power is given unto me in heaven and in earth. Go ye therefore, and teach all nations" (Matt. 28:18, 19). Mark adds a greater dimension to what Jesus commanded the disciples to do, "And these signs shall follow them that believe; In my name shall they cast out devils; they shall speak with new tongues . . . , they shall lay hands on the sick, and they shall recover" (Mark 16:17, 18).

In Matthew, Jesus had said that a sign that the kingdom of heaven had been manifested to them was his ability to heal the sick and cast out demons. Now that he has won the final victory over Satan, he gives this same authority to every believer. The fact that Christ is in charge is manifested to the world not only by our preaching in the power of the Holy Spirit, but by our ability to pray for the sick and see them recover, plus our ability to take authority over what remains of Satan's counterfeit kingdom.

I call Satan's kingdom of darkness counterfeit because of its nature and length of durability. I have particular reference to its durability.

An earthly kingdom not only concentrates on maintaining its authority, but also its longevity. This is why one of the most important things a king could do is have an heir. Today, in some parts of the world, divorce is accepted as proper recourse for a king when his queen does not bear him an heir to his throne. By having an heir, the king feels that his kingdom will be able to outlive him.

Satan's authority was only to be a temporary phenomenon in history. In Genesis 3:15, God tells the serpent, signifying Satan, that the woman's seed would be bruised in his heel, but the serpent's head would be bruised by the seed of the woman. There was no doubt in Satan's mind what this prophecy meant.

In ancient battles, the victor was able to end the conflict and manifest his victory by placing his foot on the head of the conquered foe. Satan knew that there would be One coming from the human race who would limit the extent of his authority on this earth. He would not be an angel, but he would be a man. That man was Jesus Christ. Further Old Testament prophecy stated that he would be of the tribe of Judah and of the seed of Jesse. This is the reason why Satan attacked the seed of man. Giants populated the earth as a result of angelic beings coming in contact with the daughters of men. Noah's family had not been defiled and so God preserved the human race after the flood. However, Satan continued his attack on God's nation, Israel. On many occasions, they would have been destroyed as a people, but for God's protection. Satan was going to do everything possible to keep the prophecy in Genesis 3:15 from coming to pass.

Paul tells us in Ephesians 1 that Christ's authority is far above all other rule, authority, and name both in this entire age, but also in the future age. Therefore Christ's authority has no point of termination.

The question of Christ's heirs is also solved by the apostle. He states that we are fellow heirs with Christ. Therefore, we are seated with Christ in the heavenly realm which is far above the earthly plane. It is clear that we have all of the authority necessary now to accomplish the Great Commission to go into all the world and make disciples of the nations.

What Is the Gospel of the Kingdom?

The word gospel means good news. So often people come to church and they hear everything but good news. They hear about what Satan is doing. What politicians are doing. What is happening in the world which indicates that the time of the Antichrist is near. I have seen Christians come to church happy and when they leave, they feel afraid and depressed. They have heard the bad news instead of the Good News. All you have to do is turn on a television set, radio or pick up a newspaper and you have all the bad news you need. What people in the church need to know is what the Good News is!

The Good News is that God is in complete control and we are on the winning side. Sometimes, I pick up a book and like to look at the last chapter. If I find that the book has a sad ending, I feel I had better not begin the book. Why should I read for many hours, only to be saddened at the end of the story? But as we look at the last portion of the Word of God, the Good News becomes obvious. We are the winners. Matthew 13:16 gives us understanding of how special we really are. In the context of a few verses Jesus states how fortunate we are to be able to understand the whole picture.

I think of these verses as a beautiful puzzle like the ones I used to give my children. They would take out all the pieces and spread them on the floor of our house. Certain parts of the picture were immediately recognizable, but other sections of the puzzle were not understood until you put the entire thing together. So it was with the prophets. They only prophesied in part. They gave what the Holy Spirit anointed them to say. But now that Christ put the entire puzzle together, we are blessed. That is, we can look at each part and see how it fits into the whole picture. We can turn to Isaiah and see what God meant when he gave the prophet the fifty-third chapter.

Yet, the gospel of the kingdom falls on different kinds of soil. Satan is out to take it away from us because it is the only message which exposes his total defeat by Christ and gives us the courage to fight the good fight of faith.

The word of the kingdom falls on four types of hearts.

A roadside is so well traveled that it becomes hard. A seed falling on this type of ground has little chance of becoming a meaningful plant. These people simply are not interested and they never allow this message to root in their hearts.

The stony earth indicates a group of people who hear the word, understand its implication, but will not pay the price to let the message really change their lives.

The thorny earth indicates the group who accept the word, but they are more concerned with the things of this present life, therefore it is not as important to them and it never takes root.

But then you have a group who hear the message of the kingdom of God and they are willing to pay whatever price they have to pay to bring about its fruit. They give it the priority necessary for its success and therefore bear their fruit according to the ability given to them.

The gospel of the kingdom of God has to be heard, experienced and then proclaimed. The early apostles were willing to pay the price necessary for the kingdom of God to be manifested in the early church. Rome would not have objected to just another religious sect coming out of the Jewish religion, but the Roman authorities objected vehemently to the proclamation that there was another king, Jesus Christ the Lord. Caesar was king at that time, but the early church proclaimed that he was only a temporary reality. There was another more powerful and eternal king, Jesus Christ. Then they proved that this king was in charge by healing the sick. Miracles became an obvious way of not being challenged to just argue the merits of a new religion.

The subject of divine healing is a controversial one today. I have never had a problem with divine healing because if it were not for healing I would now be a dead Buddhist. Remember, I was converted to Christianity when I was on a deathbed, dying from what seemed to be a terminal case of tuberculosis.

Yet, I realize that for many evangelical ministers, divine healing presents a theological problem. I am quite sensitive to this problem. In fact, many of our Church Growth Conferences are sponsored by pastors and churches that do not practice divine healing. In Mexico, the chairman of the Church Growth Conference which attracted 4500 Christian leaders was a Presbyterian who had a problem with the whole subject of divine healing. Many of my best friends have been taught that divine healing was a temporary need for the early church. Once the Bible was completed, healing was no longer necessary and divine healing was done away with. Although I don't agree with this theological view, I don't believe that those who espouse it love Jesus less or are second class ministers of the gospel.

I believe that we should try to keep the unity that the Holy Spirit is trying to establish in the church today, until we all agree eventually. I view differences of opinion on interpreting the Bible among sincere and genuine Christians as entering a dark room. One might come in from one door and feel his way around and say he is in the living room. I might come in from another door and say we are in the dining room. The only way we will find out is to continue loving each other until the light is turned on and then the room's function will be obvious.

Peter addresses the progressive character of revelation in 2 Peter 1:19, "We have also a more sure word of prophecy; whereunto ye do well to take heed; as unto a light that shineth in a dark place, until the day dawn, and the day star arises in your hearts." Peter says that the Scriptures are a more prophetic revelation than an audible word from the Father at the Mount of Transfiguration. This Scripture is then likened to a light which is shining in a dark place. Shining is in the progressive present tense. Progressive Greek tenses show continuity of action. That means that our understanding of the Scripture is getting brighter, and will continue to brighten until we understand it clearly at the return of our day star, the Lord Jesus Christ.

So if you don't agree with me on divine healing, don't get offended, love me—you might learn something! I hope you never have to change your mind because you need divine healing. If you already believe in divine healing, and you think that I am apologizing for it, you are wrong. I make no apologies for what I see is the trusted truth of the Word of God and a clear manifestation that the kingdom is at work in our community.

I have had literally thousands of experiences of divine healing in my church. We believe God for health for our members. But we also believe in praying for the sick and expect God to perform the miracle. We also believe in the ministry of medicine. Having a number of doctors in our church, we see them give God an opportunity to either perform an obvious miracle, or they then use their God-given skills as medical men and see God heal that way as well. God uses both. However, I believe in God for miracles in our church. This proves to an unbelieving community that God is alive and that people don't have to suffer. After all, Buddha cannot heal them. Only Jesus can heal the spirit, soul and body.

Healing and Miracles As It Relates to Church Growth

A minister once told me that healing was no longer necessary. He said to me that miracles were for a day before civilization enlightened the world to reason. I strongly disagree with him. As I travel the world, I have seen men who claim to be civilized act in a most uncivilized manner. At the end of World War II the world found out that Germany, the most educated, cultured, and scientifically advanced nation in the world, had allowed itself to perform the most uncivilized atrocities in recorded history. No, the world may be more educated, but we have seen our present age drowning in the polluted waters of pornography, filth, and perversion. In this present day, the healing power of the Holy Spirit has to be given to a sick and needy society.

In Korea we have discovered that many people who were not open to the gospel become open when they have a physical need in their body or in their family. It is well known throughout most of Korea that our church is a place where God is obviously at work. Not that we have mass healing on Sundays. But God does move in healing and people spread the word.

The Holy Spirit Is Concerned

One of the elders of my church had a crippled son. He had been a handsome young boy, but suddenly his legs stopped functioning and he had to use a wheelchair. The doctors were not sure as to his problem and told my elder that his son would have to spend the rest of his life as a cripple. For three years I prayed for him and nothing happened. I became disgusted at the devil for afflicting this boy in the prime of his life with this deforming disease. "Why am I sick, pastor?" the boy asked me one day in my office. "What sin did I commit for God to punish me this way?" I had few answers. But I reassured him that he was not afflicted by God. "This is the work of Satan. We are not going to accept this crippling disease as final. The devil is a defeated foe. By the stripes which Jesus suffered, you are healed," I reassured him. This gave him temporary hope, but after a while everyone accepted the sickness, and we loved and accepted him with his problem.

My wife and I enjoy being with our elders. We have fifty elders now and they function as a board of directors in our church, similar to the Presbyterian Congregational system. One evening we were all together in a fellowship dinner. My wife and I were sitting together enjoying our Korean food. We Koreans enjoy eating together. We eat foods that some people find spicy, but it is an important part of our social life.

"Go to Elder Kim, tell him that his son is going to be healed tonight!" The Holy Spirit was speaking to my heart. I leaned over to my wife, Grace, and said, "The Holy Spirit just spoke to me." She looked at me and smiled. Grace was named properly—she can do everything in such a gracious manner. "Wonderful," she said, not knowing what God had said. "Grace, the Holy Spirit just spoke to me to go to Elder Kim and tell him that his son was going to be completely healed tonight." With those words now out of my mouth, Grace did not change her expression too much, for the sake of the others sitting at the table. But she reached down and pinched my leg and with a much smaller smile on her face she said, "Yonggi Cho, don't you dare do that! How many times have you prayed for him? If it doesn't happen you will be the laughing stock of the entire community." My wife usually believes God with a powerful faith, but this time she had not heard the voice, so she was left to her reason.

"Do not listen to your wife. Go and tell Elder Kim that his son is going to be healed tonight!" The voice was stronger and my heart was weaker. I quietly tried to slip out of my seat. But just then my wife saw me and asked, "Where are you going?" "Nowhere," I said weakly. God knows that I did not want to obey the voice. I felt like dying. But I have learned that it is better to obey than wonder whether you should have obeyed. When you begin to walk with the Holy Spirit, obedience is very important. If you continuously disobey, the voice grows weaker until it becomes quenched and you become insensitive.

I leaned against the table where Elder Kim and his wife were sitting. In a little while Elder Kim looked up at me and asked, "Pastor, is there anything wrong? Why are you looking at me?"

I took a deep breath and said strongly, "God just spoke to me that your son is going to be healed tonight."

"Praise the Living God," Elder Kim cried out. He and his wife just sat and wept. They were crying tears of joy. Others joined them in their rejoicing, but I wasn't rejoicing, I was sick. "Why did I do that?" I asked my wife. "Because you didn't listen to me, that is why," she replied.

I always have great faith when the Holy Spirit is upon me, but after the special presence leaves, then my natural mind takes over and I regret having obeyed the Lord. Yet I have learned never to let my reason rule my heart. One must be careful not to be led by emotion, but by the Holy Spirit.

When Elder Kim got home, he expected his son to be healed. Yet his son was crawling out of bed, not able to walk. They came into his room and announced to him what I had said. But the boy was still on the floor unable to move. The parents knowing that I would never tell them something that I was not sure God was speaking, took his arms and stood the boy up. "In the Name of Jesus, you are healed tonight. God spoke to our pastor and we believe it's true. Walk!" After a few minutes, the boy began to feel something in his legs.

I could not sleep, as I lay in bed wondering what was going to happen tomorrow. If nothing happened to the boy, I was not as concerned for my reputation as for the integrity of God in our town.

At Elder Kim's house the boy was finding new strength in his legs. "I feel a tingling sensation up my legs, Father." After a few minutes, the boy began to walk. The parents rejoiced, but didn't call me.

In the morning I got word that the young man had run out of the house and began to tell all of the neighbors what had happened. All of the Buddhists and other non-Christians in the town knew the situation, and they were amazed at the power of God. Since then most of the people in that part of town have been saved because of the healing power of God. The kingdom of God had been manifested in that community and the people came to Christ.

God desires to heal, not to build up my reputation, but to glorify his name. Yet, for three years, the boy had suffered. Why? I don't have all of the answers, nor do I attempt to justify God's ways. They are totally beyond my understanding. But I do know that God can and will heal, if we trust him to fulfill his word and will be obedient to his voice.

Binding Satan

Our church believes in the existence of a real devil. We believe that he is more than the personification of evil. We believe that he is as real as Jesus. God said to Moses, "I am that I am is sending you." Satan would have said, "I am and I'm not." Not believing in the existence of Satan is being in the place where you have no defense against him.

When we pray, we have learned to use the authority given to us by Jesus. He told Peter first and then the rest of the disciples, "That which you shall loose on earth is loosed in heaven." Our people have learned that we are not wrestling against flesh and blood. Our main concern is not with the communists on our northern border. Our main enemy is with the power that is driving the Communist North Koreans. We therefore bind the power of Satan at work in our community. We can accomplish more through our joint prayers than can be accomplished through all of the arms at the free world's disposal. Moses learned the importance of prayer when he had to keep his arms up for Israel to defeat the enemy. We have the power and authority because Christ gave them to us.

A growing and active church is a congregation of believers who know who they are in Christ. They know that we Christians are more than conquerors. They know that the weapons of our warfare are not carnal or temporal, but they are mighty to the pulling down of the strongholds of the enemy. They are not afraid of the enemy, but they are aware of his tactics. They know that the warfare with the devil is real and that keeps them sober and vigilant.

I thank God that the Word of the kingdom of God in Korea has not fallen on deaf ears. Perhaps it is because we have known great suffering as a people. We have suffered two wars in the last forty years. So we don't take the promises of God lightly.

The early church also suffered. They were persecuted by the Roman Empire. They knew what it was to die for the sake of Christ. This is why Christ sent them a letter through John on the island of Patmos. The book of Revelation scares many people who don't understand its message. But as we see the whole letter in its context, we realize that Christ is Lord. Although the Antichrist might appear soon, although we may yet have much suffering ahead, Jesus Christ is in complete control and his final victory has already been won. With this strong assurance from the resurrected Christ, the early church could stand firm and finally win the victory over the persecutors. Yes, the early church conquered the conquerors. Not with chariots and horses, but with the message of the gospel of the kingdom of God. Rome fell to the Christian world, not in annihilation, but in conversion. Rome finally accepted the fact that Jesus was Lord and the Caesar, Constantine, had to bow his knees to a greater king, the Lord Jesus Christ.

The gospel of the kingdom of God should be preached regularly from every pulpit in the world every single week. People will then get excited about the Lord we serve and love.

Yes, your church can and will grow, if the sinners in the community that you serve finally realize that the God who is being worshiped in your church is alive and moving. He can meet their needs. There is never a smug person in need. Only those who don't realize they are in great need can act indifferently toward your ministry. But everyone gets into a position when they need Christ. At that time, people will know that God is at work in your church and they will come and see the kingdom of God in manifestation.

6
Church Growth and Revival

What is revival? F. Carlton Booth has given an excellent definition of this term. "In many instances the word revive, Hebrew:
'haya,' Greek: 'anazao,' means literally to come back to life from
the dead. Even when this is not the meaning, the word carries
greater force than it bears to us today for we have confused
revivalism with evangelism. Evangelism is Good News; revival
is new life. Evangelism is man working for God; revival is God
working in a sovereign way on man's behalf. To speak of holding
a revival is a misnomer. No human being can kindle the interest,
quicken the conscience of a people, generate the intensity of spiritual life, whether in an individual or in a community, in the
church or in the nation but the Spirit of God. No man can
schedule a revival, for God alone is the giver of life. But when
darkness deepens, when moral declension reaches its lowest ebb,
when the church becomes cold, lukewarm, dead, when 'the fulness
of time' is come and prayer ascends from a few earnest hearts,
'Wilt thou not revive us again: that thy people may rejoice in
thee?' (Psalm 85:6), then history teaches it is time for the tide
of revival to sweep in once more. Revival always involves the
preaching of divine judgment, confession of sin, repentance, acceptance of salvation as a free gift, the authority of the Scriptures

93

and the joy and discipline of the Christian life. While revivals do not last, the effects of revivals always endure" (*Baker's Dictionary of Theology*).

It must always be remembered that the church began as a sovereign work of the Holy Spirit. When the 120 followers of Christ waited in Jerusalem, they had no idea of what was going to happen. They were together, they were in one accord and they were expecting God to do something. Then the Holy Spirit did what had never happened before. Therefore, the church was born in a revival.

The first phenomenon which accompanied the Holy Spirit's obvious work in the lives of the faithful was given to show those who were outside the fold that God was truly working in the midst of his people. Therefore, the fiery tongues that were over the disciples were signs to the unbelievers. So the purpose of a revival, the working of God in his people, is to show the world that he is alive and cause them to hear the Good News of the gospel of Jesus Christ.

As is so often the case, that which begins with the spark of divine life, settles in the ashes of human reason. All movements begin because an idea causes people to become excited, but as is true of human emotions, excitement cannot be maintained indefinitely. During the development of a movement, men are attracted who have the mental capacity to rationalize the dynamics and develop the ideology which will give perspective to what was just motivated by excitement. When the time of emotion dies down, the movement that neglects what birthed it settles into the study of its ideology. This has been true of the church.

The Book of Acts is not a book of theology, it is a history of the early stages of the church of Jesus Christ. It clearly shows us some principles of revival.

All revivals are the sovereign work of the Holy Spirit. The third member of the Trinity is so often the forgotten person of the Godhead. We pray to the Father in the Son's name. But what about the Holy Spirit?

The first time the Holy Spirit is mentioned in the Acts of the Apostles shows us one of his most important functions. "Until the day in which he was taken up, after that he through the Holy Ghost had given commandments unto the apostles whom he had chosen" (Acts 1:2). The Holy Spirit is the Spirit of Truth.

He is the one who illuminates our minds to speak the truth of God and he also illuminates our hearts to understand the truth that is spoken.

The Holy Spirit had come upon the prophets but he had never totally filled or immersed anyone until Jesus. Now Jesus was offering what was his exclusive right to give, the baptism in the Holy Spirit. The disciples were obviously not cognizant of the importance of what Jesus was offering them when they asked him concerning the kingdom being given back to Israel. Yet, Jesus continued by showing what the effects of the Holy Spirit baptism would be. "You will receive power." This would be the effect of the Holy Spirit's filling the disciples. This power would enable the weak and ineffective followers of Christ to be strong and powerful witnesses of the gospel. The Holy Spirit not only gave the new church great power which was able to attract the attention of the unbelievers, but he was also able to break the prejudices of the early church.

As long as the church was Jewish in composition, it was able to attract many other Jews to the knowledge of Christ the Messiah. But once the church opened the doors of faith to the Gentiles, Jews hesitated to join a group that would cause them to become less than traditionally Jewish. Peter was given a vision and spoken to by the Holy Spirit. His command was to go to a God-fearing Italian named Cornelius. While Peter spoke in Cornelius's home the Holy Spirit sovereignly worked in spite of Peter's prejudice. These believing Gentiles were also filled with the Holy Spirit in the same way that Peter had experienced the Holy Spirit at the Day of Pentecost. This event caused so much uproar, that Peter had to defend himself in Jerusalem: "Forasmuch then as God gave them the like gift as he did unto us, who believed on the Lord Jesus Christ; what was I, that I could withstand God?" (Acts 11:17). Therefore, the sovereign work of the Holy Spirit was able to break through the anti-Gentile attitude of the apostles and open the door of faith to the rest of the non-Jewish world. In both instances where Peter used his keys of the kingdom to open the door of faith to the Jews and later to the Gentiles, the Holy Spirit worked sovereignly. Yet, there is another fact that needs to be seen concerning both of these events. Both the disciples at Jerusalem and the Gentiles at Cornelius's home were in an attitude of prolonged prayer.

Prayer is the key to revival. If revival is the sovereign work of the Holy Spirit, what causes the Holy Spirit to move upon the hearts of God's people bringing new power and greater boldness? The simple answer is prayer.

How many times have you spent all night on your knees before God? How often has your church called all of its members together for prolonged fasting and praying? Could this be the reason you are not experiencing revival in your life and ministry?

If this is your problem, cheer up! This section is especially written for you. You are going to find a new desire to pray. You are going to realize that the reason you have not been the kind of Christian you have wanted to be is because you have not prayed. I don't expect you to want to pray because I am going to quote verses you already know. No! You are going to want to pray because the Holy Spirit is going to touch your heart as you prayerfully read on.

In Luke, we are given a great secret, "Which of you shall have a friend, and shall go unto him at midnight, and say unto him, Friend, lend me three loaves. For a friend of mine in his journey has come to me, and I have nothing to set before him? And he will answer from within and say, Trouble me not: the door is now shut, and my children are with me in bed; I cannot rise and give thee. I say unto you, Though he will not rise and give him, because he is his friend, yet because of his importunity he will rise and give him as many as he needeth" (Luke 11:5–9). The Lord will respond to relentless prayer and will be touched by our importunity. The dynamics of that verse are important to understand.

First, the man who is requesting bread is a friend of the one who has the bread. We must not approach God as a stranger. He is our Heavenly Father and is anxious to give us all that we need. We need a revival in our lives and especially in our church. We are tired of the dead services and lifeless prayer meetings we have been having. We need a spiritual awakening. But we don't approach God as a stranger, we approach him as a friend.

Second, we are not just asking for ourselves. The man whom Jesus is using as an example has had visitors at a late hour and he has nothing to give them. Oriental hospitality demands that he feed those who come into his home. So too the church is constantly visited by hungry sinners in need of spiritual life. So many of the church's cupboards are empty and the sinners leave the church building empty and unsaved, never to return again. Our request from God is justified; we need revival for the sake of those for whom Christ died, those who have not found the meaning of eternal life.

Third, the hour is late. There is nowhere else the world can go to find security and nourishment. Only we have the ability to meet the needs of this dying world. If not us, who? If not now, when? This is the state of present society throughout the world, if we are sensitive enough to world affairs to know that the hour is late.

Fourth, the door may be shut, but it can be opened. There is a hope in the heart of the man who is requesting the three loaves that his answer can be yes. Revival is possible for every church. You don't have to be in Korea to experience revival— you may be anywhere. Like the Japanese story I shared with you before, there is never a field that is too difficult. Although the door seems to be shut now, you must believe that the God who is behind the door will open it if you will not faint but will persist in prayer.

Last of all, there has to be developed an attitude of intense desire in order for someone to persist in prayer. The man who was requesting the three loaves was afraid of losing his honor. If anyone heard that visitors to his home were not properly treated, he would have lost his honor and would be better dead. We in the Oriental world have an expression which is called, "losing your face." When you lose your face, you lose your honor. Many would rather die than lose their face. I can understand how desperate the man was. He did not want to lose his honor. Therefore, he was desperate. In order for someone to persist in the kind of prayer necessary to bring revival, he must become desperate before God.

Sometimes prosperity keeps American Christians from being desperate before God. We in Korea have experienced great human suffering—first at the hands of the Japanese for many years and then at the hands of the Communists. We know what it is to be hungry and have nakedness and shame. We have learned to pray, not from the comforts of our living rooms, but out in the fields. In like manner the Chinese Christians have learned how to pray in the woods and forests, in caves and cold basements. If caught, they could be killed for praying, but they have learned that without prayer they cannot survive.

In *A Tale of Two Cities,* Charles Dickens, the famous nineteenth-century English writer, tells us that the spirit of revolution manifested itself in two ways in the French and English cultures of the early nineteenth century. The bloody revolution that France experienced was prevented in England not by the political differences of the two nations, but by the fact that Great Britain experienced a Holy Spirit revival through the ministry of John Wesley. Wesley was a priest in the Church of England in the eighteenth century. He and his brother Charles experienced a personal spiritual awakening. At a time of personal adversity, John Wesley went to his knees before God, and God touched him in a special way. His eyes were opened to the biblical truth of sanctification and personal holiness. In 1739 he began to share what the Holy Spirit had revealed to him. This new understanding caused him to suffer great persecution with other awakened ministers in the Anglican Church.

By the middle of the eighteenth century, his teachings were being spread all over the British Colonies, including the United States. Most of the proclaimers of this new method of Christian living were laymen.

The Wesleyan revival in Britain caused such a change that it is credited with saving the masses from revolt and bloodshed. It also spurred on education for all the people plus a more humanitarian attitude toward the poor. Historians must recognize the influence of the Methodist revival on present Western culture.

Today, one of the largest denominations in the world is the Methodist Church. However, many of its members do not realize how the movement began. It began in adversity and grew because of revival. In much of the old Methodist literature which still remains, we can read about the all-night prayer meetings and vigils of prayer. No wonder that as you travel through America it is hard to find a town or city without a Methodist church.

Much can be said about the revivals in Wales, India, Latin America, and America; but one fact remains constant. No historic or modern revival has ever taken place without people realizing that they must pray. I don't mean sentence prayers or moments of prayer or words of prayers—but I do mean long and concerted prayer and fasting before God. I can honestly say that we are experiencing a genuine revival in Korea. At this time, the church is growing at four times the birth rate of our country. This means that in twenty years, should the Lord tarry, we are going to have a population which will be over 80 percent Christian.

We must remember that Korea was traditionally a Buddhist nation. Winning people to Christ has not been easy. It is much easier to win a convert who has been raised in a traditional Christian atmosphere. After all, the West has long been exposed to the gospel. Yet, in Korea we are seeing a great harvest among nonbelievers. They are coming to the God of the Bible. This is truly the work of the Holy Spirit.

As I write this page, we now have over 330,000 members in our church. By the time this book is published, the membership will possibly be much greater than 350,000. We are seeing approximately 10,000 converts joining our church every month. Would you not call that a real revival?

How have we maintained such unusual growth in our local church? The real answer is prayer. Every Friday night we have an all-night prayer meeting. We literally don't have enough room for all the people who want to come and pray. We pray for our nation and its leaders. We pray for the gospel to be preached throughout the whole world. We pray for our Lord and Savior Jesus Christ to return. We pray for a revival to begin in America and Japan. In fact, we pray for thousands of letters that are mailed to us from our New York and Tokyo offices. We sing, we worship and we hear the Word, but mostly, we pray. The easiest way for the revival we are now experiencing to stop is for us to call off our weekly all-night prayer meetings. But we have no intention of calling them off. We must pray.

Prayer Mountain

Several years ago we bought a sixty-acre tract of land only six miles from the North Korean border. We originally bought the land to use as our own church cemetery. My mother-in-law, Dr. Choi, was fasting and praying and suddenly the Lord spoke to her, "Build a special place dedicated to prayer." "We must develop a prayer mountain," she told me. "This is the most difficult time for us," I said. "We are in the midst of the worst financial crisis of our church's history," I reasoned. But my mother-in-law seemed not to be concerned with the rationale for postponing Prayer Mountain. I too felt strongly that our church needed a place to go and totally concentrate on prayer and fasting. So, with no money, we began to build Prayer Mountain.

Originally we put up a tent for people to pray together. Then along the hillside, we built prayer grottos—that is, small caves right into the earth with a little mat and a door. Here, people could lock themselves in with God and seek him with no distractions. After a while, we found that there were more people wanting to fast and pray than we had room for. We then constructed a cement block building capable of housing three thousand people.

In 1982, we counted 630,000 people who had checked into Prayer Mountain from all over the world. One of the people whom I remember going to Prayer Mountain was a lady who had a crippled son. "Dr. Cho, please pray for my son," the woman implored me. "He is completely crippled. His legs are mangled and now the paralysis is getting worse."

"You must go to Prayer Mountain. There your son will be healed in seven weeks," I told her. The lady went with her son faithfully for six weekends, but nothing had happened. On the last day of the seventh weekend, God healed the young man and now he is completely whole. Word spread throughout the country that if you need a special miracle, Prayer Mountain is the place where God is moving. I am not saying that everyone who goes to Prayer Mountain will be healed. But I am saying that I know of many people whom God has healed at Prayer Mountain.

As a leader, I must set the example for my congregation. If I don't pray, they won't pray. I have my own prayer grotto at Prayer Mountain. Whenever I have a problem that I can't find a solution for, I check into Prayer Mountain and lock my door. It often takes hours to get all of the things out of my mind. The best way to do that is to tell everything to the Lord. I have learned to be honest with God.

If someone has hurt me, I tell God about it.

Not long ago a man wanted to destroy my ministry. He sent spies into our church to hear me speak. Sunday after Sunday, he would come and listen to every word I said, hoping to catch an exaggeration. Every testimony I shared, he would check out carefully. One day I spoke on the importance of honoring our parents. This subject had particular importance to our Oriental Christians because of our Confucian past. Confucius taught a system of ethics, not a religion. His ethics are still popular throughout the Orient till this day. One of his most important teachings had to do with honoring our ancestors. In some parts of Asia, people still worship their ancestors. Christianity cannot be accepted by many because it does not teach what the position of one's ancestors are. I then shared how the Bible taught us to honor our parents. This did not mean to worship them but to simply hold them in high esteem. God did not want only to honor them while they are still alive, so we could assume that it was not a sin to honor them even after they had passed on to glory. Abraham was still held in high esteem as the father of faith.

This gave the spy the ammunition he was looking for. He publicly accused me of being a false teacher and teaching idolatry. This accusation reached the newspapers and I was thrown into the middle of a controversy. Some told me to sue him in court, but I felt I should go to Prayer Mountain. At Prayer Mountain, I told the Lord the whole story. I shared with God how angry I felt and what I wanted to do.

After several hours in prayer, I heard God speak to me to forgive the man. So I forgave him. Did I want to forgive him? Yes. Why? Because God had placed forgiveness in me. This did not happen all at once. It took hours for the Lord to heal my heart of all the hurt and bitterness, but finally I felt forgiveness come into my heart and I could honestly forgive the man.

You see, I was healed at Prayer Mountain. Yes, I was healed of a greater illness than paralysis. I was healed in my heart of bitterness. As I share with my people what God has done in me at Prayer Mountain, it encourages others to go and get their needs met.

Why should ten thousand people pray and fast at Prayer Mountain? Don't they have televisions to watch and good restaurants to eat in? I am sure that this question has been asked by many people. We Koreans are just like other people. We enjoy a good meal in a restaurant and have many of the finest restaurants in the world. We have television and radio. In fact, Seoul is now one of the most beautiful and modern cities in the world.

Now that we are getting ready for the Olympic Games in

1988, there is a great construction boom taking place all over Seoul. So people don't go to Prayer Mountain because they have nothing else to do. They go to Prayer Mountain because they believe that God is there to answer their needs. This does not mean that God can't answer them anywhere. That is not the point. God is everywhere. But you can't always find a place that has been dedicated to God, where you can get alone with God for many hours plus join thousands of other people who have totally dedicated this time to seeking God.

People have to be motivated. Prayer Mountain would be empty today if I did not emphasize the importance of prayer on a regular basis. So, if you were to come to one of our Church Growth International seminars in Korea, you also would see our new ten-thousand-seat auditorium full of those who are seeking God. Our floors are heated so that you could place your mat on the floor and pray with everyone else. I am sure that you would never be the same. You would also see the thousands of prayer requests translated into Korean being prayed over. In fact, I don't know of requests that are more prayed over than the prayer requests sent in from our New York office.

Now that we are having these thousands of people accustomed to going to Prayer Mountain, I can charge them with special things to pray for. For instance, when President Ronald Reagan was shot, I had all of the Christians praying for him day and night. We were so pleased when I got a phone call from our New York office that the president would survive.

We also prayed about the war that took place in Lebanon. I believed that God would intervene and stop the needless bloodshed among the Lebanese people. Now that the PLO is out of Lebanon, we are praying for a revival to start in the church there. With all of the suffering in Lebanon for the past eight years, that nation is ready for an old-fashioned Holy Ghost revival that will heal all of the bitterness of the past and cause men and women to turn to God by the thousands.

For the past two years we have been praying for Japan. With our own television program we can reach seventy million Japanese people. We are in continual prayer at Prayer Mountain for a revival in the Japanese church. I am sure we are going to see a great work of the Holy Spirit in Japan soon. You must realize how hard it was for me to go to Japan. After knowing about the millions of people massacred by the Japanese before 1945, I had a great hatred toward the Japanese people. However, God healed my heart when I confessed my sin. I now travel to Japan every month. In fact, last year we had a great crusade in Yokohama with Pat and Shirley Boone. This is only the beginning. Why do I have so much faith for Japan? We are praying at Prayer Mountain daily for a great Japanese revival.

As I stated before, I am on television in the United States. With all of the Christian television programs in America, I found it hard to believe that I too would be on American television. But after the letters that I am continually receiving from American Christians, I now know why I had to go on television in the United States.

After traveling throughout America for many years, I have noticed that so much of American Christianity is straying from the path that God meant for it to follow. I have noticed that there are a few places where Christians really know how to pray. But for the most part, the American churches don't have a real prayer ministry. I hear people speaking about revival, but the revival has not yet come on a large scale. No people has ever given more for the preaching of the gospel than the people from the United States of America. No country has ever sacrificed its own to save others from the oppression of tyranny more than the American people. Why, then, is there not a nationwide revival? The answer is prayer.

Through our television program, we are encouraging people to pray. We are teaching the importance of prayer on an individual and church basis. We have also mobilized our prayer troops to pray every single day for America. You see, if America fails, the gospel will be hurt in the whole world. Therefore, we must pray that a great revival springs up in every part of that great country. We are now praying that churches will start to grow in the United States as never before. There is no reason why New York City should not have a church of 50,000 members. Why doesn't Los Angeles have a church of 100,000 members?

Are there too many other churches in your community? No, not if there is a real revival that will cause churches to get on fire and see thousands saved in every state. If we could have several large churches here in the city of Seoul, there are not too many churches. After all, we have the largest Presbyterian church in the world. No, the reason why we can have so many large churches is that we are experiencing a genuine revival from the Holy Spirit. The reason why God has opened the doors of heaven is that there are too many Christians who have made up their minds that we need revival and will not leave God alone.

Recently, I received a report that there are now over fifty million Christians in the People's Republic of China who are meeting in cell groups. I cannot share too much openly, but I do know that they are now praying for revival in the United States as well. Since they do not get much news from the outside world, they believe what the Holy Spirit shows them. He has been telling them that American Christians need to learn how to pray. So they have been praying for their American brothers, that a great awakening might begin.

This is the hour for a revival in your church. Your community is never going to be the same. They are going to see the Holy Spirit at work in your church and are going to be drawn by the Spirit of love that is going to be emanating from every member. I sincerely believe that God led you to this chapter because now you are getting a fresh desire to begin praying as never before. I don't care how many years you have been a Christian, you have needed to get this fresh desire to pray. You also are getting a new vision of how your church can begin fasting and praying on a regular basis. How do I know this? Because I am praying as I write this chapter.

How do I pray?

I have alluded to several principles in this book already, but now I will give you my seven basic principles of prayer:

1. Get still before God.

The Psalmist wrote from personal experience in Psalm 46:10, "Be still and know that I am God." We have to recognize that God has not given us an option but a command. Unfortunately, most of our inexperienced praying is talking *to* God. There is nothing wrong with that, in fact, it is a good way to get still before God. As I shared before, I have learned to tell God everything that is bothering me. This causes me to run out of steam and get still before him. We must also remember that prayer is a dialogue, not a monologue. Therefore, when we pray, we should expect to hear and not just speak. God is not the author of confusion but of peace. God best speaks in an attitude of peace.

2. Get into communion with the Holy Spirit.

We have already looked at 1 Corinthians chapter 2. We have seen how only the Holy Spirit knows the mind of God. He is the one empowered to take a quieted spirit and put it into communion with God and reveal God's plan for us. This is true in both the specific as well as in the general direction that God wants to take us.

I begin by speaking directly to the Holy Spirit. I say, "Dear Holy Spirit, I need to know what my Father wants me to do. Please open my spirit at this time and reveal to me what he would show me that I may glorify my Savior Jesus Christ." I continue, "I love you, Holy Spirit. You birthed me into the body of Christ. You have filled me. You have given me your gifts so I may bless this world. Dear Holy Spirit, show me what I need to know."

One day I had a problem. Someone had asked me where God's residence was. Was it in heaven? I answered yes. But where is heaven? If someone in Australia looks up to heaven, then someone in Alaska must look down toward heaven. I must admit that I did not have the answer at that time. So I got up on the next Sunday and said to my congregation, "Next Sunday, I will give you God's address." Everyone was so happy. So I went into my prayer grotto and got my spirit quiet before God. I then began to fellowship with the Holy Spirit. After all, he knows everything. As I continued to pray, the Holy Spirit gave me the answer. I could not wait for Sunday. I got up before my people and said, "Today, I am going to give you God's address." Everyone got out their pencils and paper and looked at me. "God's address is in you!" As I continued to preach, people were blessed by the reality of the indwelling presence of God.

3. Develop your visions and dreams.

I have stated before how important it is to have a vision from God. This is particularly important in prayer. I recently heard a psychiatrist say that the subconscious mind is mostly affected by imagery. If a person sees something, it will affect the subconscious mind much more than just hearing it. This is why we have so many instances of people praying as they look at something. When Daniel was concerned about the future of his nation, he prayed toward Jerusalem. John at Patmos was told to see what God would reveal to him. I am sure that John sat by the edge of the waters at Patmos, where you can almost see the shores of Ephesus. His revelation began by revealing the condition of the churches that had been under his care before he was banished by Rome to Patmos. Joseph saw a vision before it became reality. Abraham had to look at something as God was promising him. He looked at the land that he would inherit and that image stayed in his heart. He became filled with that vision until it became a reality.

A woman came to me and said, "Dr. Cho, please pray for my son who is not a Christian. He is living a very sinful life. I have prayed for years, but nothing happens." "Go home and start to see him as a Christian as you pray for his salvation," I told her. "Yes, picture him in your mind as he would act and look if he were a believer." After several weeks the same lady told me how difficult it was in the beginning to pray for her son the way I had told her to pray. But then, she changed her attitude and started viewing him as a Christian. She would picture him going with her to church. She would imagine him reading his Bible and praying. Then, she was so happy with this new vision of her son that she forgot to continue praying for him and began thanking God for his salvation.

Not long after she started thanking God for her son's salvation, he asked her to go to church with him. That Sunday, he gave his heart to the Lord and is still serving God.

A man in my church had a business that was failing. He came to my office and asked me to pray for his business. "I don't know what is wrong, pastor," he said in tears. "I have tithed regularly. I give to the poor and try to live a Christian life. But my bakery is failing. I would hate to go bankrupt because it would not be a good testimony in the community. I have witnessed to so many of my customers. So, if I fail, they will laugh at my Jesus," he continued gripping his handkerchief in great grief.

After praying for him, I taught him the principle of visions

and dreams. I said, "Go back to your bakery, Mr. Ho. Begin
to see its success. Start to count the money in the empty cash
register and look at all of the people lining up outside to get
into your crowded store." After telling him that, I prayed again
and sent him on his way. As he left he looked at me in a slightly
puzzled way but tried it anyway.

In just two months, a smiling Mr. Ho returned to my office.
"Dr. Cho, it worked. I didn't understand what you told me. I
thought you were crazy, but you are a man of God and I believe
in obeying my pastor. My wife and I now have a check to give
the church." I looked down and was amazed to see a check
for one thousand dollars. This was his tithe.

4. Take authority over the devil in your circumstances.

You must remember that you are seated with Christ in heavenly
places. Paul tells us that Christ's throne is far above all principali-
ties and powers. You have a right to see the answer to your
prayers fulfilled. The devil has no place in your business. But
as a deceiver, he will try to occupy territory that does not right-
fully belong to him. Therefore, take your rightful authority in
the name of Jesus and rebuke the devil—he must flee from your
circumstances.

5. Keep an accurate record of your requests before God.

Know when you have prayed, what you have prayed for—
and write it down. This way you will not have to depend on
your memory. You can also hold before God the unanswered
prayers and remind him of what still needs to be done. I guarantee
you will praise God for the answers once you realize how many
of your prayers are being answered. So often we pray but forget
what we pray for. When the answer comes, we don't realize
the faithfulness of God.

6. Praise God in advance.

Remember, God calls those things which are not as if they
were. God sees you and me complete in Christ. With all of our
shortcomings, with all of our sinful thoughts, God is rejoicing

over us with singing. "The Lord thy God in the midst of thee is mighty; he will save, he will rejoice over thee with joy; he will rest in his love, he will joy over thee with singing" (Zeph. 3:17).

I can just picture the mighty God of the universe singing over me and you. Now if God can see us as complete in Christ, why can we not see God's work complete already? Therefore, we rejoice even before God's answer becomes obvious.

7. *Pray without ceasing.*

How can I pastor a church so large, travel all over the world, write books, have a television ministry on two continents and still pray all of the time? Why not? What is prayer if not communion?

I have learned over the years to have my spirit poised in the proper direction. I can be in the middle of a dinner party, surrounded by many people and still have my inner being poised upward. I tell the Lord daily, "Dear Lord, I have to go to this dinner with my wife. I will be in fellowship with your people. But, at any time, I will be open to go aside with you. Just because I'm busy, don't hesitate to draw me aside. Please, Lord, I am in an attitude of prayer, even though I'm busy."

I think our Lord appreciates that kind of consideration. Jesus was continually in fellowship with his Father. He never said anything unless he heard the Father say it. He never did anything unless he saw the Father do it. Therefore, it is possible to be continually open to the Father.

I have shared with you the seven principles that I use in my personal prayer life because I desire for you to develop a prayer life as well. If you already have a prayer life, then I know you did not mind my sharing this with you. If you don't have a prayer life, then the time to begin is now.

Revival will never come into your life and ministry if you don't pray. Your people will never begin praying unless you do.

"Oh Holy Ghost, revival comes from Thee. Send a revival, start the work in me. Thy Word declares, you will supply our need, for blessing now, oh Lord, I humbly plead." This old verse portrays the attitude that God desires that we all have toward revival.

Planning in a Revival

In this important chapter on church growth and revival, I have stressed the importance of perceiving a revival, praying for a revival, and persevering to a revival. Now, I need to address the important subject of planning in a revival. Why should you plan? There is a simple answer. God has never done anything without a definite plan. When he instructed Moses concerning the tabernacle, he gave Moses clear plans. The temple was built by following the clear plan God had given. The early church grew according to the plan of God. Yes, from creating the universe to the salvation of your soul, God has followed a clear plan. Therefore, why should we build our local church without a clear plan?

How can we plan for a revival?

I have already stated that revival is the sovereign work of the Holy Spirit. So you cannot plan for a revival. But you must have a plan in a revival.

I am taking it for granted that you are now believing God for a fresh working of the Holy Spirit in your life and church. Why should you pray if you don't believe God will answer? But if you do believe that God is going to answer your prayers and revival is going to come to your church, then expect hundreds and even thousands of souls to be added to your assembly. Now the obvious question arises. What are you going to do with hundreds or thousands of new members? How are you going to care for them? Where are they going to sit? What training program has been developed to get these new converts motivated and trained to reach others? The obvious problem arises—that is, many churches are praying for something they are not prepared to handle.

Just because God does something sovereignly does not mean he is going to maintain it without your cooperation. Remember, God has chosen you as his instrument in your community. You must be prepared for the answer to your prayers for revival.

Why We Haven't Planned Before

Evangelical preachers have traditionally not planned the growth of their churches carefully. What would happen to your government if it did not have a plan or a budget? The fact is that the business of the church has been run in such a way as to insure nongrowth.

I desire the return of our Lord Jesus Christ. I believe that he is coming soon. I work day and night with the hope that Jesus will find me laboring faithfully in his vineyard when he comes. But I also realize that faithful Christians have been waiting for almost two thousand years for the return of the Lord. He has not come. This means that the Lord will not return until the proper conditions are realized in this world. Jesus said in Matthew that the gospel of the kingdom would have to be preached in the whole world as a clear witness before the end of the world would come. This means that the Lord will not return unless everywhere, all men are given the opportunity to either accept or reject the Lordship of Jesus Christ. Since over 80 percent of all those who have not heard the gospel live in Asia, I am particularly challenged by that verse in Matthew 24. I believe that pastors who do not plan because they believe that the Lord is coming right away are being disobedient to the Lord's command. Luke reveals Christ's command to his disciples: "And he called his ten servants, and delivered them ten pounds, and said unto them, Occupy till I come" (Luke 19:13).

The Greek word used and here translated "occupy" is the word, *pragmateomai. The Theological Dictionary of the New Testament* commonly referred to as "Kittel's," states that this word is only used in the New Testament in this particular verse. The word literally means to do business, to make a profit. It is not a passive word, it is an active word. Classically, the word was used in reference to moneylenders. This command reveals the attitude the Lord expects us to have here on this earth until he returns. I find it interesting that the English word, "pragmatic," finds its etymological roots in this Greek word we have just considered.

Therefore, our attitude according to our Lord's command, should be the same as the ancient moneylender. We should be interested in making a profit for the kingdom of God until our Lord returns. We have been given the capital, the gospel of the kingdom of God. We know the marketplace, the hearts of sinful men. We have a secure bank, the church of Jesus Christ. Therefore, we should be seeing an increase. Yet, to solidify our increase and insure a continual return on principal, we need to plan carefully.

Another reason for lack of planning is the fact that many pastors don't have realistic faith.

In some minds, faith is a surrealistic entity, ethereal in nature. Now I consider my faith to be transcendental in nature. That is, it goes beyond the limits of my experience, similar to Kant's understanding of knowledge; I am also a very practical man. I realize that in order for me to best accomplish the purpose for which I have been called by God, I must exercise practical faith.

Hebrews tells us that faith is substantial. Jesus also described faith as personal, "According to *your* faith" (Matt 9:29, Italics mine).

Paul tells us that each of us is granted faith in a certain measure (Rom. 12:3). Therefore, we find that when we pray, we must pray in the measure of faith that has been granted to us specifically.

For example, if you have a church of three hundred members, don't start praying about increasing to ten thousand members. You have neither the experience or the inner workings of the Holy Spirit to handle such a large responsibility. This does not mean that in a few years you won't have that kind of faith, but it does mean that at this present time you must strive for something that is within practical reach. Start praying for a congregation of one thousand members. Am I limiting God? No. God cannot be limited. But I understand that God desires to work through you and you must realize your present faith capacity.

Set Realistic Goals

Let us take a pastor who has a congregation of three hundred members. Set a definite goal of one thousand. Place that goal before the Father and begin to dwell on that goal. Become obsessed with the idea of one thousand members. When you preach on Sunday, see one thousand members in front of you. When you have done that, you are ready to start planning.

Leadership Training

Your future leaders are in front of you now. The only problem is that you have not recognized them. Watch for the men and women who are faithfully attending every Sunday. They are already manifesting an important quality of future leadership—faithfulness.

In most congregations, there are usually just a few people who do most of the work. These people may be busy already, but when you want something done, they are always willing to do a little extra. These are leaders in the making.

Don't make the common mistake of calling together the most successful business people in your congregation and ask them to become lay leaders. Often, the most successful business people will not be willing to devote their time to church work. This does not mean that God will not use successful people, but they should be chosen on the basis that they are already displaying the qualities I have already stated.

Share your vision and goal with these potential leaders. Get them to start praying for revival with you. Give them each a special aspect of responsibility for the future growth of the church. A special aspect of responsibility means to get each one to pray for a specific part of your church. For example, you will need larger facilities. You will also need a larger budget. Begin to share with them the importance of developing a cell system. Most importantly, instill a burning desire within them for the salvation of lost souls.

One of the problems you will face is a general lack of genuine desire for soul-winning. We have developed an old concept of people going out into the street corner and passing out tracts to all who walk by. This is not wrong, if God leads you to pass out tracts or preach on the street corner. However, with the growth of religious cults, many people are apprehensive about those peddling religious materials on the street, and your leaders may feel hesitant about doing that type of evangelism.

Another problem that you will face is this. Most people who are active in a church are looking for fellowship groups with the purpose of becoming more spiritual. This means that they are not too anxious to win souls if it is going to keep them from growing in the Lord.

One of the truths that must be instilled in your future leaders is that the way to become more spiritual is not just to read the Bible and fellowship with other believers. No. The most effective way is to become a father or mother in the Lord. If you are a parent you know this immediately. Remember when you had your first child. You took on the responsibility of another human being. You found that you simply matured almost overnight. Now, you could not just be concerned about yourself. You had to learn how to give as never before. This is also true of those who become spiritual parents. You find that you have to study more because now you have someone who is depending on your teaching. You have to pray more because you must have answers to the never-ending questions of the new convert. There also comes a new freshness and excitement to your spiritual experience because you now have a vicarious understanding of the new birth all over again.

Once your people understand that it is in their best interest to lead people to Christ, you will find many more genuine soul-winners. I have discovered a simple principle in life. No people will be motivated to do anything over a protracted period of time unless they believe it is in their best interest to do so. Therefore, I don't try to fight what is natural to all men, I simply use that principle for the glory of God.

Lay Out the Long-Range Plan

After careful and prayerful consideration with your faithful leadership, you need to lay out the long-range plan before the people. This should not come as a surprise to anyone. You should have been building interest in your congregation all along. Your sermons should have had a definite purpose. You should have been building a growing excitement concerning the future. Now there comes the time to lay out the plan.

How long a period should the plan cover? I usually lay out a five-year plan to my people.

In 1979 I laid out a clear goal of 500,000 members by the year 1984. I know that it was the will of God. We had all prayed and considered the plan carefully for a long period of time. At that time, we only had 125,000 members. The plan was divided into several parts. By 1980 we would have 150,000 members.

By 1982 we would have 200,000 and by 1983 we would have 300,000 members. We would complete our new facilities during that year and have capacity to seat at least 30,000 in our main sanctuary and another 30,000 in our many chapels tied to the main sanctuary by closed circuit television. This would give us a total of 60,000 per service. By continuing our present seven services per Sunday, we would be able to seat 420,000 people by the end of 1983. In 1984 we would be able to add other ancillary facilities giving us a capacity of 500,000. I can now say that by the time this manuscript is complete we will have 300,000 members. Our building program is continuing as planned and, if anything, we are ahead of schedule.

Everyone knows where we are going. We are building a church of 500,000 members. Will I stop at that figure? Of course not. But I am only concerned with the goal and the plan that God has placed before me. If he has a larger goal, then he will reveal it later. But you must begin where you are. An old Chinese proverb says, "A journey of one thousand miles begins with the first step."

Budgeting

Most churches have a budget. They figure what their expenses are going to be and then they figure out what it will cost every member of the church to meet the expenses. Money is raised through canvassing or pledging during a fund-raising function. Yes, I believe in budgeting in faith.

If God is going to pour out his Holy Spirit on your church to cause a revival, you can expect new souls. With the additional membership expected you will need more staff and larger facilities. Therefore, if God has given you a clear membership goal, then you must figure on a budget to meet the greater needs of your growing congregation. You will need more Sunday-school rooms. You will need more office space, and so on.

You therefore need to have a faith budget. Trust God to show you the amount of what it will take to meet the needs of an expanded ministry. I believe that God has all the money we need to fulfill his plan. Once your people stop viewing giving to the church as a spiritual tax, you will see your people starting to give in faith. Once the congregation catches your vision they will want to participate in the fulfillment of that vision. Eventually, the larger congregation will be able to shoulder the increased burden of your church's increased budget. But as in a growing community, you must plan your finances with the realistic factoring of growth.

There is an office in our church where we have our church graphs. We have a graph showing the increase of our membership. There is also a graph where we show the increase of our finances. At a glance I can see whether we are on target or ahead of schedule. With the recent recession we had fallen a bit behind our target goals, but this only caused us to pray more and now God is meeting our targeted funds.

The kingdom of God is not inferior to the kingdoms of this world. Jesus said, "For the children of this world are in their generation wiser than the children of light" (Luke 16:8).

If all governments and major corporations have long-range planning and budgets, then why should the children of light function in a less businesslike fashion?

We are entrusted with the most important development in this world. The church of Jesus Christ is not a secondary instrument to save this world. It is God's primary instrument. In fact, God has no plan B. God only has plan A, the church of Jesus Christ. Therefore, it behooves us to plan clearly and effectively for the great revival that is about to come into our world.

Pressures of Revival

Finally, I believe one of the most important things I can share with you in this revival chapter is how to cope with the pressures of revival. If you were to realize the great pressure that will come upon you once revival comes to your church, you might halt your praying at once. Yet God has placed a great desire within you for the Holy Spirit to move in your life and church, and you will not stop. However, I have had twenty-five years of experience as a pastor and I believe I can help you avoid the mistakes I have made. But I am consoled by the fact that it is one thing to make mistakes, it is quite another to learn from them. I have learned what I have learned the hard way.

There are many areas that I could address on this important subject, but I will briefly address only five.

1. Revival and pressures on family relationships. Your family is the most important group in your life and ministry. I find that my wife is the key to whether I can succeed or fail. If she is behind me, she can cause me to succeed. If she loses interest, then she can cause me to fail. Women are motivated differently than men. Most men are motivated by their work, but most women are motivated by their relationships. Their most important relationship is the marital relationship with their husbands. Although in today's society many women have to work and develop careers in order for the family to survive financially, they are still motivated by their relationships more than by their jobs. This was discovered in a poll taken last year in the United States. I believe that this is true universally.

When revival comes to your church, you will see a great increase of souls. Many members will be added to your church. There will be even greater demands upon you than there are already.

The Book of Acts shows us the beginning of a great revival. Peter saw three thousand respond to his first sermon. Later, another five thousand were added to the church. There was such a spirit of excitement that people were willing to sell their possessions and share the proceeds with all of the members of this new family unit, the church. Yet, after a period of time there arose a great contention between the Greek Gentile women and the Jewish women in the church. My point is that while the energy and emotion of the revival were still fervent, people were willing to overlook the prejudices and problems that were before them. But once the fervor died down, these problems surfaced and caused great turmoil.

I have discovered that the great demands upon my time cannot be allowed to keep me from maintaining a close relationship with my wife. She has to come first. One way to accomplish this is to have her work with me. My wife runs the music program of our church. She has two masters degrees in music and is well qualified.

Grace is also the head of our publishing house. She takes care of all of our personal book business. She also travels with me when I go to major crusades and conferences. She is a vital part of my ministry. Eve was created as a helper who was a suitable (translated "meet" in the King James Version) helper for Adam. So when a wife feels a part of what her husband is doing, she will be able to take the untold pressures that a revival will bring without complaining. Your children cannot be brought up hating the work that took their father from them. Sometimes this latent attitude will surface in later years and cause them to avoid church involvement themselves.

What is the answer?

The answer simply is to learn to budget your time effectively. Set priorities on your time. Your family comes after your relationship with God. Then comes your church responsibilities.

2. Maintaining a proper and disciplined attitude. Success is as difficult to cope with as failure, but its pressure upon our characters is much more powerful. Failure causes a man to think about what went wrong and then make the corrections necessary in order for the same mistake not to be repeated. Success focuses our attention on the positive aspects of our work. It brings accolades from others. Sometimes it causes us to think that for some reason we are special people, perhaps beyond God's rules that apply to others. This brings untold pressure upon the foundations of our integrity. This is why I spent the first part of this book stressing the importance of developing personal resources.

Therefore, in a revival, it is extremely important for us to guard our personal moral lives. We must watch out for signs of moral slippage. We should not turn from our old friends who are willing to disagree with us and tell us when they feel we are making a mistake. It is a mistake to surround ourselves with people who always agree with us. That is what happened to King Saul. When he was small in his own eyes, the Lord made him king; but, when he was puffed up with pride, the Lord took the kingdom from him and gave it to another.

3. Maintain a spirit of forgiveness. As you see your membership grow you will also see the problems in your church grow as well. Problems in the church are caused by people. The larger the church, the more problems there will be to deal with. You can't always please everyone. If you spend your time trying to please the Lord and walk in the peace of the Holy Spirit, then you will eventually please those in your church who are also in accord with the Holy Spirit. The more popular you become, the more open you will be for others to mark you out for special criticism. Therefore, you will find a bitterness and anger trying

to root in your heart. Remember that the heart is the place where you will find the devil trying to begin to destroy you. If your heart attitude begins to sour, you will see your health and physical strength begin to fail as well.

The best way to combat this problem is to practice forgiveness. Forgive everyone who hurts you whether they ask for forgiveness or not. Remember that Christ forgave humanity at the cross even though there was not one voice being raised asking for forgiveness.

I was born in a difficult time in Korean history. We were not a nation. We were under the oppressive hand of Japan. Against their will millions of Koreans were carried as slaves to Japan. We were not allowed even to speak the Korean language. So, as a child, I grew to hate the Japanese.

Eight years ago, the Holy Spirit started dealing with me about Japan. I told the Lord, "Dear Lord, I know that my attitude toward the Japanese people is not correct, but I can't help how I feel." Yet the Lord had a special way of healing me. I was invited to minister to a group of Japanese pastors.

Arriving in Japan, I felt very uneasy. This was the land that had taken away our name and language, had punished our patriots, had burned our churches and massacred our Christians who had remained faithful to their religion and nation. When I got up to speak, I tried to say some nice things about Japan but I could not. I began to weep. A deep silence filled the audience of ministers. I then looked up and confessed how I felt.

"I must confess that I hate you all. I don't hate you personally, but I hate the fact that you are Japanese. I know that this is wrong, but this is the way I honestly feel. Won't you please forgive me? I am repenting of my sin and ask you to pray for me." With those words spoken, I simply bowed my head and began to cry aloud. When I looked up, I saw that all of the ministers were crying also. After a few minutes, one of the ministers stood on his feet and said, "Dr. Cho, we as Japanese take full responsibility for the sins of our fathers. Will you please forgive us?" Then I came down from the platform and threw my arms around the man who had just spoken. "Yes, I forgive you and I commit myself to pray for you and Japan." I instantly felt healed of the bitterness that I had felt since a child. I was free.

God has now given me a promise that ten million Japanese are going to be saved in the decade of the eighties. I now go to Japan every month. I have a nationwide television ministry to Japan. I am trusting God for a great revival to spread throughout all of Japan. I saw all of this take place because I asked God to heal me of my bitterness.

4. Practice moderation. With the success of a growing church comes the great temptation to think of yourself as a successful businessman and then start trying to live on a scale similar to others who you relate to as successful as well. Money can be the greatest hindrance to maintaining the growth of your revived church. I have learned to abstain from the mere appearance of evil. I constantly get envelopes full of money. I never even open the envelopes. I immediately hand them over to a church secretary who takes the money to the church treasurer. I will not accept money for any ministry given to me personally. I give everything to the church. This way I cannot be accused of taking money from people in order to pray for them.

I also live a moderately comfortable life. My wife and I have all of our needs taken care of, but we don't live a life style that will in any way hinder the effectiveness of my ministry. This does not mean that we don't believe in prosperity. We do. But I believe more in the continued effectiveness of my ministry to the church, nation and the world.

5. Keep yourself from developing a sectarian attitude. We as church leaders have to always remember that we are not in competition with the ministers of other churches, but we are in a life-and-death battle with the devil for the souls of lost men. We cannot have an exclusive spirit, but we must maintain a spirit of love and cooperation with the rest of the churches in the community. This year alone is a perfect example of how we all must work together in our city of Seoul, Korea. In 1982, our church grew from 200,000 members to 300,000 members. Yet, we gave 15,000 new converts to other churches. Then, we started another two churches in Seoul and gave them 5,000 converts to start with. We have a good relationship with the Presbyterian, Methodist and other churches in our community. Although we are the largest church, we are not the only church in the city— and I certainly am not the only minister in the city!

The world needs to see that we love one another. They need

to see that Christ has only one Body and that Body is not divided. They will never believe in our message if they cannot perceive our love.

This is the last great move of the Holy Spirit before Christ returns. I believe that. I believe that the emphasis is now on the local church. The world's needs are going to be met by a revived clergy and laity all working together for the evangelization of the world. Revival must come to the local church in order for the church to be ready for the great task that Christ has placed before her. Are you ready for the pressures that revival will bring?

If the answer is yes, then you are trusting in the grace of God to guide you into what is coming.

7
Church Growth International

There is no question in my mind about the fresh emphasis the Holy Spirit has brought on the subject of church growth. Church Growth International is not a denomination or a movement limited to one particular type of church. Church Growth International is an organization created to serve the needs of all church leadership throughout the entire world.

Years ago, as I was traveling back from a speaking tour in Europe, the Holy Spirit spoke within my heart, "Go home and begin a new organization dedicated to the emphasizing of church growth!" "Lord, how is this possible? I am a Korean. Who will listen to me?" was my surprised reaction to God's command.

"Father, all big organizations begin in America. They have such talented ministers. I am from the Third World, the developing world," I continued, finding my heart suddenly fearful as I faced this new challenge. I looked out of the window of the Lufthansa jet and wondered how I could begin another organization and still maintain my busy schedule as pastor of what was then a church with a congregation of 50,000 members. But the words kept ringing in my heart, "Develop a center for training at the church. People will come from all over the world to see church growth for themselves."

I settled the issue by saying to the Lord, "Father, we need a facility on Yoido Island (where our church is located) and that is going to be very expensive. If on Sunday, as I share this new vision, the people respond with pledges and gifts of one million dollars, then I know you really want me to build a center for church growth in Korea."

I shared the vision with our leadership and we agreed to lay it before the people. That Sunday we asked for an offering including pledges for the building of a World Mission Center. After our last service, our church treasurer came into my office with a smile. "Pastor, we have received pledges and gifts totaling exactly one million dollars." God had spoken and he had confirmed his word with the resources necessary to begin construction of our new facility.

The Lord also sent back an American missionary who had helped me in the past. He labored with me until this past year when Dr. Il Suk Cha took over the responsibility as coordinator of Church Growth International. I was blessed to see my old friend and elder take on this new responsibility as a volunteer. Bringing with him many years of business expertise and a sincere desire for world evangelization, Dr. Cha is organizing C.G.I. into an effective tool in the church growth movement.

C.G.I. is not only responsible for the developing of training sessions in Korea, but also the organizing of C.G.I. conferences throughout the world.

Two years ago in December, we were invited to come to Mexico City. The Reverend Daniel Ost, missionary statesman and pastor of three large Mexican churches, invited me to come. The executive committee was chaired by a Presbyterian pastor and it consisted of most of the evangelical churches in Mexico. When I landed in Mexico City I immediately felt right at home. I sensed the spirit of revival in the atmosphere over this, one of the largest cities in the world. In fact, Mexico City now has a population of over seventeen million people.

When I approached the platform, I was so tired from my travel that I told Rev. Ost, who was my interpreter, "Danny, I won't be able to speak more than thirty minutes. I am really tired." Yet, when I saw the ballroom of the Hotel Mexico filled with more than ten thousand Christian leaders, when I saw the enthusiasm they had, their deep love for Jesus and their great

Latin hospitality, I found a new strength to speak for two hours! Pastors came from twelve countries, mostly from Latin America. They came with an expectancy I have found in few other places in this world. Oh, how I love the Mexican people. They are so warm. They loved me although I was obviously different than they. But most important, they came to the teaching sessions with an attitude of faith and expectancy. We are still getting reports from Mexico concerning the lasting effects of our Church Growth International conference. It is my sincere belief that the conference has had a deep and lasting effect on Latin American evangelism.

With the economic problems that have surfaced in Mexico, the time is ripe for a great move of the Holy Spirit. Pastors there are now building their churches around the cell system. They have caught the vision of prayer and revival, and they are working to meet the needs of the people. This is the hour for a Mexican visitation of the Holy Spirit. Therefore, we are praying for this great and pivotal nation.

Church Growth International's Leadership

Church Growth International is guided and directed by an international advisory board of successful pastors. These are men who have proven ministries and are interested in devoting their time and energy to seeing the principles of church growth taught throughout the world. They also help me raise the funds necessary to continue to minister in C.G.I. conferences all over the world. In fact, we are also developing a C.G.I. membership of clergy and laity to stand together in reaching out to countries that cannot afford to pay for one of these conferences themselves.

At our annual meeting last year held in Australia, we decided to concentrate on teaching the neediest of countries. Without exception the response is always positive. But we have been hindered from reaching many countries through lack of funds. "Why don't you take up offerings in Korea for these needs?" I have heard this question asked quite often. Due to strict currency regulations, money cannot be taken out of Korea in any significant sums. We have to rely on the host country and those that are catching the vision of church growth in the developed world.

My desire is to go into countries that have extended to us

emotional pleas for help. India has begged us to come and hold a C.G.I. conference. We could easily have 100,000 pastors and church leaders attend. But there are no funds now. But I have every hope and confidence that God is supplying the resources necessary to reach out to countries such as India, the Carribbean Islands, and the African countries that have invited us.

Church Growth International's Direction

I have received direction from the Holy Spirit concerning the manifestation of the kingdom of God in this earth. The church is to be revived before the second coming of the Lord. Although there is going to be a falling away, this is the pruning of the tree, not the cutting off of living branches. The purpose of pruning is to bring new life. While we are seeing many churches empty, many pulpits remaining unfilled because of a lack of interest in the ministry, there is a fresh life developing. Those churches that are truly preaching the gospel of the Lord Jesus Christ in the power of the Holy Spirit are being revived.

To fulfill her mission on earth the church needs to touch every sector of society. She must minister to government leaders as well as peasants. She must be the example of justice and mercy. She must meet the human and physical needs of people as she tries to save their souls. In order for the church to accomplish this great goal, she must have direction. The church needs to know where she is going and how she is going to get there. She needs to let the world know that we are not giving up on this world—that while the god of this age is at work, we have made a fresh commitment to reach the believing community in a more comprehensive way.

Our Plan for Reaching Nations

C.G.I. is meeting with evangelical Christian leaders from all parts of the world. Our plan is simple.

1. We judge the general composition of the national organizing committee. We desire to touch the whole church and not just a segment of it. We are not sectarian in nature, but we desire to work with people who are genuinely interested in evangelism and church growth. We see that the committee is composed of

respected and representative members of the evangelical church in that nation. We believe that the principles that I have shared in this book will work for any believing church. Therefore we do not want to limit the conference to one particular denomination.

2. We then work closely with the local committee of church leaders to see that the arrangements which are made are made in faith. In February of 1982 we went to the Philippines. I was told that this was going to be our worst C.G.I. Conference. There was not enough money. There was not enough time to plan carefully. Yet, our people, working with the local committee headed by Methodist Bishop Castro, had planned in faith. They had rented the largest auditorium, seating 30,000 people.

Although I had been warned by some of my closest advisors that I had better cancel the conference, I knew I had heard from God. So I was not surprised to see the results of the Manila C.G.I. meeting. Our party was met at the plane as it came to rest on the airport tarmac by an official delegation including government officials. We were quickly escorted into transportation provided by the government to our hotel. In fact, every time we traveled, we were provided a motorcycle police escort. Five thousand pastors and Christian leaders registered to attend the complete seminar.

At night, the auditorium was full of people. I preached the gospel every evening and invited people to make decisions for Christ. A total of eight thousand people made decisions for Jesus Christ during that crusade and conference. The government was so receptive to our emphasis on the growth of the church that they gave us a state luncheon. President Marcos thanked us for coming to the Philippines. He acknowledged the importance of the church in his country as the most effective organization which is bringing an era of social and spiritual renewal to his country.

During the week that we spent in Manila, we saw a whole nation's church leadership touched by the power of God. They left the teaching seminars with a new confidence and hope for church growth.

3. Speakers are chosen who can share experientially as well as theoretically about church growth. I am indebted to the many pastors who have traveled at their own expense to share the principles of church growth in our C.G.I. conferences. Pastor

Thomas F. Reid, pastor in the Buffalo area of New York, has taught with me at many church growth conferences.

Having put the principles which I have shared in this book into operation in his own church in Orchard Park, Pastor Reid speaks from a platform of experience. His cell meetings have been the key to his success. One of the cells was directed by a Jewish convert whom Dr. Reid had trained. The cell started reaching out to the Jewish community in the Buffalo area. Soon, they found the need to buy their own facility and purchased a former Jewish funeral home. Now, on Friday evenings many believing Jews meet together and share their new-found faith in their Messiah. They are also mobilized to try to win other Jews to Christ. The cell is still a vital part of the mother church, but they have followed the principle of homogeneity which has proven extremely successful.

One of their cells has a commitment to reach the needy inner city of Buffalo. They have developed a growing ministry to a part of that city that other churches had neglected. These former poor people now have new hope. Their financial condition may not have changed dramatically yet, but they have discovered that poverty is a state of mind and not a balance in a checkbook. As Christians we cannot be poor. We are children of the King. Although we may not have all of the world's goods, we are heirs with Christ of all of the riches of the Father. Once their mental attitude and self-image changed, their material condition began to change as well.

4. Practical topics are chosen. I believe that Christian leaders everywhere are interested in practical answers to their problems. They are not much interested in theory; they want answers that work, taught by people who have proven these answers in actual experience. Therefore, the subjects that we teach are very practical in nature.

In one of the seminars I taught in the United States, I began the sessions by asking a question, "How are you going to convince your church that they need to change their present thinking and move in a different direction?" Immediately, I could see interest on the faces of my audience. The men and women who had registered for the conference had traveled many miles to find new direction for their ministries. After sitting through seminars and question-and-answer sessions, they were excited about church growth in their own congregations. During the night, I am sure many had worried about how they were going to sell this new direction to their boards. Now my question had sparked intense interest.

I then shared for two hours on how to practically motivate their people. I used many examples in my own church as well as those from some of the most successful pastors in the world. We keep our sessions geared to meet the practical needs of evangelical leaders.

5. We always work through the local church. Although it would be easier and more practical for me to set up our own meetings with an advance team trying to get the cooperation of the local churches, I always work through the local church. This is not to criticize the ministry of many of the great evangelists who go into a city with their own organization sponsoring the meetings. I believe the pastor and the evangelist must work together for the great goal of world evangelization. If evangelists waited for the cooperation of pastors in some communities, they would never preach in that area. Unfortunately, many churches are still in competition with each other and have not caught the vision of church growth. However, as a pastor with a ministry geared toward building up the Body of Christ, I must work through the local church. This maintains my integrity with the local church leadership and makes the work of Church Growth International more effective.

6. How is C.G.I. financed? Every religious organization is presently in a fund-raising program today, or so it seems. The recent recession has hit the world a hard fiscal blow which has not missed religious groups. However, our trust and confidence is in the Lord of people, not the people of the Lord. Yet, in order for Church Growth International to continue to exist outside of Korea, we need to raise a considerable budget.

When we are in countries that are developed economically, we usually take up a love offering for C.G.I. which will help finance our outreach into the underdeveloped world. The churches in this part of the world are in the greatest need.

Our television ministry in the United States, once it starts to pay for itself, will then raise missionary funds to reach the whole world with the message of church growth. This is the only hope the world has. We must have revitalization of the local church, a revived ministry in order for us to ever see this world effectively reached for Christ. I personally have committed my resources for this and God is now joining many churches and businessmen to us for the purposes which I have already stated.

God has given us C.G.I. members in Singapore, Europe and North America who are catching a new vision. Although the group is now just starting to grow, they are committed to the goal of world evangelization.

7. Another resource is Church Growth International Publications. Until last year, our missions magazine was called *World of Faith*. This magazine is now called *Church Growth* and it is presently published quarterly. In this publication, we continue to share effective principles of church growth. We have regular articles written by successful pastors in every issue, sharing their particular prospective on church growth. Informative reports from all over the world showing what God is doing through C.G.I. are an important feature of every issue. The magazine is presently written in English, but we hope to create other editions of this important periodical as well.

We publish the magazine in Korea with the help of a dedicated staff. One of the most popular sections of the magazine is an updated report of the progress of the Full Gospel Central Church.

8. The effects of Church Growth International. Through the ministry of C.G.I., we have seen a significant number of churches literally become more effective in reaching their communities for Christ. Pastor Robert Tilton of north Dallas recently shared with me his story. Pastor Tilton is a member of our C.G.I. television board along with some of the most successful ministers in the United States. He is a strong supporter of the C.G.I. ministry.

A few years ago, Pastor Tilton and his wife moved into a suburb of Dallas with a vision of building a church to minister to the needs of that great city. I met Pastor Tilton two years ago and found him to be a man of vision. In a matter of just a few years, he has built a church with a congregation of seven thousand members. His television ministry, Day Star, is now syndicated in several cities throughout America. Once Pastor Tilton caught the vision of church growth, he began to run with it. Now he has developed six hundred cells throughout Dallas. They are presently in a building program which should be completed soon with a seating capacity of five thousand people.

"My goal is to have a congregation of 100,000 members by 1986," he stated with sincere determination. I believe that there are going to be many congregations of that size in every major city in the world when pastors catch the vision of church growth.

Pastor Stanley of the First Baptist Church in Atlanta, Georgia, came to Korea two years ago with his associate. I did not realize that Dr. Stanley was a noted leader within the Southern Baptist denomination. When he came to Korea, he kept a low profile. He simply said, "We have come to pray and to learn." I was impressed by Dr. Stanley's humility and graciousness. Yet, upon his return to the beautiful city of Atlanta, he began to put the church growth principles he had learned in Seoul into practice. The results are quite impressive. In the past two years the church has doubled in size. This is an outstanding achievement even by Baptist standards.

Van Nuys, California, is a lovely part of America. The First Baptist Church in that city is pastored by Dr. Jess Moody. Pastor Moody had been a successful pastor in Palm Beach, Florida, when the Lord called him to his new California parish. The church had been through some difficulties and the attendance was way down. Dr. Moody began to seek the Lord concerning a new direction for his church. Through much praying, the Holy Spirit spoke to Dr. Moody's heart to become familiar with our ministry. Since then, we have become close friends and Dr. Moody is on our C.G.I. advisory board.

Through the cell system, their congregation has grown to one of the largest in California. But their vision does not stop there. Dr. Moody believes in touching the lives of each person in his large church. So the cell system was instituted. Now the cell leaders are sharing the love of Christ individually to both motion picture stars and the working class people of Van Nuys.

Our desire is to touch churches from all denominations that have a sincere desire to evangelize their communities and therefore grow dynamically.

Whether in North America, Latin America or Europe, the story remains the same. C.G.I. is being used by God to a greater degree than I ever imagined. Perhaps my vision was too small in the past, but now I have a greater vision than ever. My vision for C.G.I. was influenced last year by our crusade in Singapore.

Singapore is one of the most beautiful places in the world.

Prosperity has come to this small island in the past few years. The country is primarily Chinese in origin but there is also a large Indian and European population.

Last year, the business leaders of Singapore got a vision from the Holy Spirit. They were to sponsor a national crusade to reach all of Singapore. They rented the local soccer stadium which seats 70,000 people. One business leader alone, Mr. Wy Wy Wong, paid for the total advertising in every newspaper in the country. The committee was composed of pastors, professional people and businessmen. These men and women had one thing in common. They had a burning desire for revival in Singapore, which has a small Christian population.

Night after night, for five straight nights, the rains came in torrents. But by six o'clock every evening, the sky would clear and we were able to have large crowds gather to hear the gospel.

The total count of people that came forward to accept Christ amazed me. I repeated nightly. "Please, only those who want to accept Christ as their personal Savior for the first time in your life, only you come forward." Yet, we counted more than 50,000 people making decisions for Jesus Christ.

My meetings with the local church leaders were very encouraging as well. I believe that Singapore is going to be a bastion of Christianity in the future. It has people who are committed to church growth. My hope is that they will use their newly found prosperity to more effectively reach other Asians for Christ.

Whether in France, where we saw ten thousand people come, or in Denmark, Finland, West Germany, or Japan; we have seen C.G.I. as an effective tool in the hand of God to reach leaders and church members with new hope and vision.

In January of the year, I spoke at a Faith Seminar in Winter Haven, Florida. Pastor Quinten Edwards hosted this conference in his beautiful new church which seats over four thousand. Dr. Edwards is also a member of our C.G.I. television board. While at this seminar, the Holy Spirit spoke to me, "My son, you are to touch every pastor and church leader in this country. Although I give you permission to speak to all Christians, your main task is to share from your heart those things that I have spoken to you with pastors and church leaders." On Friday night, we announced that on Saturday morning, I would be sharing with only pastors and leaders. At nine in the morning, I saw two hundred pastors gather at the Cypress Cathedral eager to hear the Word of God. At that meeting, I shared for two hours. I noticed that there were few with dry eyes as I gave them the Word. Some told me that the anointing with the Holy Spirit was so powerful, they could hardly stay in their seats.

This has changed my strategy. I will now have a special session with church leaders everywhere I go in America. I also will pray for each one of them, praying that God will impart vision for church growth.

I believe that we have only seen the beginning of Church Growth International's effectiveness. I can see reaching every country on the face of this earth with the gospel of Jesus Christ. I can see every pastor who loves Christ in this world receiving a fresh vision from the Holy Spirit and beginning a revival in the local church.

Is the vision too large? No! To get the job done, we must see a thriving church in every local community on earth. Because God has allowed me to build the largest church in the history of the world, I can speak with experience and authority.

The same God who took a boy dying with terminal tuberculosis and healed him, the same God who saved that young man from Buddhism, the same God who caused him to build the largest church in a Third World country—that same God will help this ministry in cooperation with other ministries dedicated to world evangelism.

We must all work together to bring back the King of kings and Lord of lords.

8
Church Growth and the Future

Several months ago, I was flying from a speaking tour when I noticed a gentleman across the aisle of the plane. He seemed to be playing with his watch for a prolonged period of time, so I got up, went past his seat and noticed that he was playing a video game on his watch. This caused me to think as I headed back toward my seat.

We are now in the era of greatest change in history. Technology has developed so quickly that it is impossible to predict what life will be like in the next ten years. The technological revolution has affected the lives of almost the entire world. In Korea, we can watch events happening halfway around the world as they actually take place.

Sociologically, the world is much more different than I ever thought possible. Not only in America, but in much of the world, people are being categorized in mere numbers. This has caused a general depersonalization in society. Computers have taken over many jobs previously held by people. Words like bytes, chips, and software are becoming integral parts of our language. Consequently, the dehumanizing of modern society has brought numerous problems that the church must address. Alienation, loneliness, and depression are common symptoms of our modern

133

way of life. In order to grow, the church must know the problems of modern men and women, and show them the answers.

Fear has been with us for a long time, but never more intensely than it is today. Our ability to obliterate the planet by pushing a button has caused much of the world to live in fear. Historically, we have always had tragedies. However, today's instant communication systems have caused us to be aware of more catastrophes, wars, earthquakes and revolutions than ever before.

Another fact that is challenging the church today is the world population explosion. By the year 2000 more people will be alive on this planet than all of the people that have ever lived and died combined. Yet, only a small percentage of the world population has most of the world's resources. Inequities exist everywhere. Injustice, oppression, and inhumanity are on the increase. Where do the representatives of God stand on these important issues? Is the church relevant to today's society? These questions are asked of us all the time, not just by liberals, but increasingly by other evangelical believers who are both sensitive and concerned.

Alvin Toffler, a well-known American author, recently wrote a book that addressed the sociological changes taking place and tried to give us an unusual perspective to them. In this book, *The Third Wave,* he analyzes the past in terms of waves of human experience. He uses the metaphor of the wave because waves blend into each other so they are often coexistent, yet they remain distinctive.

The first wave was the agricultural society. This wave lasted thousands of years. The second wave was the industrial revolution which began in the nineteenth century. The third wave is the wave that we are now experiencing and it is the wave of the future. However, this wave is not easily defined in Toffler's book. Although I found the book interesting, I also found that the author could not predict the future with the same clarity that he described the past. It is always easier to be an historian than a prophet. It concerns me that many ministers of the gospel consider the changes that are taking place to be evil. They forget that God is in control of the future of this world, not the devil. All of the present and future problems that we experience are not necessarily obstacles but opportunities. The church cannot be a victim of change; she must be the guiding light in the midst of change.

There is no question in my mind that the most widely read book in the history of the world has the answers in principle form to the problems facing the last part of the twentieth century. However, God's truth, the Bible, needs to be interpreted so that the world can understand its message. Jesus did not quote Scripture to the world. He took God's Word and interpreted it to meet the needs of the people to whom he ministered. To grow, a church must meet the needs of society. It must answer questions and heal the spiritual and emotional sickness that plagues all people. The church in the future will have to deal with the problems that face her in the present, and then effectively proclaim and live in the reality of the Good News. To do this, we must identify the basic problems facing us today. We must also remember that the world cannot give answers to man's basic needs; it can only ask questions. Our responsibility is to listen to the questions carefully, analyze them prayerfully, and give the answers humbly.

Even science has no answers for the human needs of society; however, it is helpful in giving us information and data. When scientists try to assume the role of prophet, they usually make greater leaps of faith than Christians do. Robert J. Oppenheimer, theoretical scientist and one of the fathers of the atom bomb, tried to step into the role of prophet in the 1960s. He stated that the future would be bright because of the advancement of science. Scientists would be able to solve man's problems in the future. Yet, twenty years later, we have more social problems than Dr. Oppenheimer ever imagined. The truth is that scientists approach human maladies from a wrong presuppositional basis. Since man's basic problem is spiritual, the answer must have a spiritual basis. Only those of us who are in communion with the Holy Spirit can effectively deal with the problems of the world. In doing so, we then fill the void of human need and become more relevant in the minds of our community.

Our Message. Our message must be presented clearly and concisely. We need to address issues that are prominent in our community's thinking. We must ask the questions that people are asking and then our replies must answer the questions honestly and specifically. No other group has a source book that is eternally true. We are the custodians of the manufacturer's handbook for better living. Our Creator has communicatd to us the rules that work. Yet, the world is not aware of the clear directions God has given us. I heard a saying once that I have found to be true: "If all else fails, read the directions." Society is not working, but where are the directions? They are in the Holy Bible. The Holy Spirit is waiting for us to communicate with him, so that he can take the eternal truth and make it specifically applicable to our present problems.

Successful Message. A basic tenet of success used in business is, "Find a void and fill it efficiently." This same principle will work in building a successful church. Find the void! Everyone has one. Every town has something that it is concerned with, whether it is unemployment, inflation, energy, crime, politics, or something else. Fill the void! Commune with the Holy Spirit and find out what he has to say about the problem. He will direct you to the correct scriptures. How often do we read that Jesus picked up an Old Testament scroll, read a chapter, then began speaking on the verses which had been read? Not often. Why? Because he knew how to get people's attention.

What is the use of having the answer if people are not asking the questions? We must address the questions which are being asked. Jesus dealt with issues like taxes being imposed by the Romans and attitudes toward those who were poor and mis-treated. He then gave the answers from the Father and backed his words with the Scriptures. As we look at the ministry of the New Testament church, we see a group that was not full of intellectuals, had few financial resources, but was able to change the course of history. This is the kind of a church that can, at the end of this age, meet the needs of humanity in its most trying hour. What is needed in the church is the completion of the restoration process. That is, the rebuilding of the church to its initial balance, ministry, truth, unity and power.

Eschatologically, I believe in the truth that there is a period of time coming when the world will experience great tribulation. I believe that the Antichrist will be manifested and men will receive the just recompense of their actions. Yet I believe that the church will be strong before the end of this age and will be able to carry out the original vision given by Christ to take the Good News to all nations before the end of the age. I am, there-fore, optimistic as to the future of the church.

Can we use the resources that are at our disposal to preach the Word effectively to the largest potential audience ever assembled in the history of the world? Is it possible for us to minister the truth in the power of the Holy Spirit and, as a result, more people will be in heaven than in hell? The answer must be yes to both these questions.

To accomplish these great goals, we must see the restoration process completed. What do I mean by restoration process?

After it became acceptable and empowered, the church also became corrupted. In European history, the resulting degeneration of the church caused what is commonly referred to as the Dark Ages. A change came as Martin Luther rediscovered the doctrine of justification by faith and it was brought back to the church. John Wesley was used by the Holy Spirit to show another aspect of the reformation and restoration process—emphasizing the truth of sanctification and holiness. The Holy Spirit and his gifts were brought back to the church in a fresh way in the beginning of this century. Now, we are seeing the restoration of the local church and its growth as an integral part of the restoration process.

Pastors are now discovering that their main function is to train the laity for ministry. They are establishing the house-to-house as well as the temple ministry. Believing and planning for renewal, they are preparing for the greatest revival in the history of the world. There are at least five areas that I believe we must see restored in the church in the near future.

1. The Balance of Reason and Spirituality

Men are naturally drawn to two different areas of understanding: the mystical and the rational. A neurosurgeon once told me that the two parts of the brain which control the emotion and the reason work differently in all of us. Therefore, we are attracted to the mystical aspect of Christianity, or what I will call the spiritual or the rational. This dichotomy of perception has existed since Aristotle and Plato. Yet, in the New Testament church, Paul could present the basic doctrine of the faith, while John presented the experiential relationship with Christ. There was a balance of theology and experience.

The Catholic church was influenced in these two differing areas by St. Augustine and St. Thomas Aquinas. Augustine was the bishop of Hippo in the fifth century. He developed a Platonic philosophy based on Christianity. Faithful to the Scriptures, he wrote on subjects such as the Trinity, the church, and the kingdom of God. He particularly emphasized that the enlightened soul of man was his main motivational force rather than his reason.

Living in a different era, Thomas Aquinas (1223–1274) revived Aristotelian epistomology. He discounted man's intimate relationship with God through divine enlightenment and relied on reason to prove God's existence. His belief that God can be proven through reason affected the church at that time and brought about the scholastic era of the thirteenth and fourteenth centuries. The early reformation movement was influenced most greatly by the teachings of Calvin and Luther.

Calvin, although most influenced by Augustine's concept of grace, still relied heavily on reason to develop his theology. Yet his reason was used within the framework of the Scriptures. He was able to influence and, in turn, totally change his society by the continuous teaching of the Word of God. Yet there was little emphasis on the experiential aspect of Christianity.

Martin Luther, also, was orthodox in his teaching, yet he often referred to his own spiritual experiences.

Present-day evangelical Christians are faced with the same choice regarding their faith. However, what is coming to the believing community is a proper balance between reason and experience. We at the Full Gospel Central Church are endeavoring to reach a proper synthesis between experience and theology. I have seen the importance of both in the past fifteen years. Having come from a Pentecostal background, I have been greatly influenced by experiential Christianity. This caused the reality of the divine presence to become meaningful not only to my mind but also to my heart. Yet I noticed that many who relied too heavily on experience tended to become unstable in their Christian walk. This was because experience is not a constant. It is based on human emotion which is neuter from a moral point of view. In other words, emotion is neither good nor bad. It is a phenomena of life that can be the basis of great pain or pleasure, depending on the stimuli.

The church originally was not begun as a result of a group of theological lectures; it was begun as a result of a divine intervention with emotionally uplifting results. Yet the church grew because of the continual teaching of the apostles and the practical application of that teaching in the daily fellowship and prayer of the new saints.

The emphasis of our church has not forgotten the experiential, particularly the most important experience which is the new birth; but we have taught our people how to live and how to witness. Our services are such that anyone coming into our church for the first time would not be uncomfortable. We have tried to maintain a balance between strong teaching and experience. Yet, I have also noted that, in many churches that place emphasis purely on teaching and that negate experience, the members tend to be dry and lifeless. Prayer, which is the key ingredient to revival, is not emphasized with the fervency that we read about in the Scriptures. What is needed is the freedom from the fear of the unknown and trust that the Holy Spirit will not bring confusion but peace.

I recently enjoyed a visit to the First Baptist Church of Van Nuys, California. For a number of weeks, Pastor Jess Moody taught on praise and worship. Although the church is not charismatic, they sing and worship God in such an enthusiastic manner that you would think you were in a Pentecostal service. Dr. Moody, a scholar with a long and faithful reputation within his own Southern Baptist denomination, believes that the Scriptures concerning praise and worship cannot be removed from the Bible. Since the evangelical churches believe in the Scriptures, enthusiasm belongs as much to the evangelicals as it does to the Pentecostal community. The strong growth in his church is not only attributable to the cell system but also to a lively and vibrant worship service on Sundays.

Spirit without Word causes fanaticism. Word without Spirit causes "stagnaticism." A proper balance of both will cause dynamic church growth.

2. Restoration of Ministry

A contemporary problem within the church today is an erosion of confidence among the general public toward many in positions of leadership within the church. Newspapers attack the ethics and credibility of the clergy with seeming impunity. Many of the best-known religious leaders have come under unusual attack recently concerning moral and business affairs. Unfortunately, this affects all of us who are in the ministry.

Although most of what is reported against God's people is not substantiated by facts, Satan has used this recent barrage to discredit the church in general. The cynicism which has developed within the general public is not new. In the Middle Ages, the European community developed a similar attitude toward the clergy. This helped motivate the Reformation. What is needed today is a new reformation and it must begin within the leadership of the church.

The prophet deals with this very problem in Ezekiel 34. This chapter corresponds to Jeremiah 23. God rebukes the shepherds of Israel in the strongest terms. The basis of his judgment is laid out in four parts.

1. God holds the leadership responsible for the safekeeping of the sheep.
2. Proper care of the sheep will keep them from going astray.
3. Proper feeding will provide safety.
4. The root cause of the problem is the shepherd's concern for his own needs and not the needs of the people.

God's answer is explicit.

David would be raised up as the shepherd and God would be more evident to the sheep. At this point, the people would be blessed and well fed. What is needed in this latter part of the twentieth century is a restoration of ministry. The word minister means servant, not ruler. The basis of our authority is not judicial but voluntary. People follow my leadership not because they have to, but because they want to. What causes 300,000 people to desire to follow my leadership as pastor? Simply, they know that I am their pastor because I serve them. How can I serve that many people? Because David (the Lord Jesus Christ) is working through me. Therefore, I cannot take personal credit for the success which Christ so richly deserves. He is the Shepherd. I am the undershepherd whose job is to carry out his instructions.

The fact that we're simply the people's servant must be carried out in actions and not words:

1. Our attitude cannot be haughty, we must be humble.
2. Our life style cannot bring our motives into question.

3. Our ministry cannot be geared to build our own personal profile.
4. Our resources cannot be used to build monuments to ourselves.
5. Our time cannot be spent in activities and involvements that don't directly benefit the church.
6. Our prayer life must be maintained so that the Chief Shepherd can actively and continually direct us.
7. Our desires must be purified from all pursuits that are not of the kingdom of God.

Following the seven principles listed above will not prevent us from the attacks of Satan, but they will prevent justified attacks. As we remain faithful to Christ, he is obligated to justify himself. We therefore don't need to justify him.

Just as the sixteenth century brought about a new ministry that became the example for others to follow, so also I see a new clergy developing in these last days. Their desire is for the sheep, not for themselves. Their goal is the building of the kingdom of God, not their own kingdoms. Their source is the Holy Spirit, not just their own ideas. This will cause a new and fresh credibility within each community among those who are sincerely looking for the reality that only Christ can give.

Therefore, I am optimistic concerning the future of the church at the end of this age. We have the example of the early church which was not perfect but was empowered. We have two thousand years of church history which can help us not to make the same mistakes. And we have the promise of Christ's first miracle, which is that Christ has saved the best for the last.

3. Restoration of Truth

To understand the increasing importance of the role of balanced ministry of the church to the world, we must understand where twentieth-century man is going.

As I traveled last year through a prominent city in the West, I went into an art museum. Although I'm usually too busy to go to museums, I was curious to find out what artists were conveying in the 1980s. I turned into the section called Modern Art. I then studied what seemed to be irrationally painted lines on canvas. "Is this art?" I asked myself. "My youngest son could paint better than this," I continued. Yet, rather than just being critical, I began to think about what I had experienced as I traveled back to my hotel. It is too easy for Christians to be critical of the world today and judge it by our standards. If we have been given grace by God to live, think and act as Christians, then why should we be so quick to judge the world, if they have not been the recipients of this grace? No, the responsibility of God's servant is not to pass judgment on the world system, but to bring God's truth to the unregenerated in an understandable and loving way.

It is not difficult to see that the world as we once knew it has changed. We only have to turn the dial of our radios and we run across what is presently called, "the new sound." If we can bear to listen for a few minutes, we realize that what we are hearing is no longer melodies and harmonies, but sheer noise. The rules that used to govern musical composition have systematically been broken in the desire to obtain freedom from them. The underlying thread of what is behind our new art and music is a growing sense of extreme skepticism—not just skepticism about God, but basic skepticism about the concept of truth. In other words, the general disorder which is growing in most areas of human expression is an attack on the basic quality of order itself. To understand this, we must understand the relationship between truth, order and rules. Rules exist to maintain order. Order exists because of man's basic concept of truth.

In the past, musical composition was orderly and conveyed meaning. J. S. Bach composed his music with great symmetry. There was a beginning and an end. Visual arts conveyed meaning as well. The great masterpieces could be appreciated because the observer understood immediately the subject of the painting. Also the painter displayed his subject in such a way as to leave the person moved with a particular understanding or feeling. In such a way this painting conveyed meaning. What brought the dramatic and puzzling change? What is driving the continuation of the destruction of order in our society today? In my opinion, it is an attack on order brought about by a skepticism concerning truth.

A skeptic is a person who no longer believes in the universality, integrity and objectivity of truth. Truth is, therefore, made a subjective reality. The skeptic's statement is, "What is true for you is not necessarily true for me." To the skeptic, truth is no longer universal, it loses its meaning. Since truth, according to the skeptic, is no longer meaningful, it loses its integrity. And because it is no longer objective, it can be made personal and subjective.

He can then justify his ethics as being situational. That is, what is right may change depending on the circumstances. Since artists and musicians are the obvious interpreters of the prevalent philosophy of the day, they paint and compose today to convince present society of the reality and authenticity of their philosophical position.

In my understanding of this new point, I must state that this position of skepticism is not new. Pyrrho, an ancient Greek philosopher, was the first known exponent of this philosophy. Thus this position is called "Pyrrhonism" among philosophers and theologians. What is our answer?

Although the person espousing this view is not new in the world, what is new is the wide scale acceptance skepticism has had within the Western intellectual community. We in the East are just being affected by it. If we can judge by recent history, in the near future the church will be dealing with it on a much larger scale.

When truth becomes relative, it ceases to exist. When I say, "This is true," I am not just stating my opinion about something which, of course, is subjective. I am relying on a universal reality which substantiates that statement. This means that, with no exception, that statement is always true. Although some modern philosophers claim that statements can only be universally true in the exact science of mathematics, others state that experience and logic can be referred to as well. For example, there are now more than 300,000 members in our church in Seoul. That statement is true. It can be verified, but it will change in one week. Therefore, it is not universally true. "The earth is basically round, not flat." That statement was true before Columbus sailed from Spain to the New World. It is true now. And, unless there is a destruction of the globe, it will be true in the future.

What has brought about this skepticism?

Two great wars in Europe within a time span of just three decades caused great devastation in Europe. The devastation was not just material and social, but also intellectual.

In the seventeenth and eighteenth centuries secular society began discarding its faith in Christianity. Instead, particularly in the nineteenth century, the intellectual community began to have faith in man's ability to create a just and lasting peaceful society through using logic and reason. This predominant view in philosophy was shared by many theologians as well. Man through medicine would conquer all disease. Through science he would be able to answer all of the mysteries of the universe. Once all the questions had been answered, mankind would be able to create peace on earth. The attitude toward religion was that it would fade away as all ancient myths had disappeared from the scene. Therefore, man had confidence in himself.

The Far East was much more structured in its sociological framework. Confucius taught a system of ethics which pervaded most Oriental societies. Due to our perennial overcrowding, we in the Orient had to learn how to get along with each other. Therefore we adopted a system which governed our actions in our family life, business, and politics. Buddhism was more philosophical in Korea and Japan than religions in Southeast Asia.

Yet World War II shattered many of our ideas and customs. America was the new conqueror. She did not come to the Far East to colonize as Great Britain, Portugal and Spain had done, but she helped us rebuild and tried to teach us a love for freedom and democracy. Therefore, in our part of Asia, we began to look to America for a new social and intellectual order. We learned English in order to communicate with our new Big Brother. It seems to be a lesson for modern history that ideas begin in Europe and take several decades to travel across the Atlantic Ocean. Once they become a part of the American culture, they are transported by films, television and literature throughout the rest of the developing world. After World War II particularly, the skepticism which had been developed began to grow. Secular existentialism, not to be confused with the existential theology of Kirkegaard, was promoted by a number of philosophers, such as Heidegger, Sartre, Camus and Becket of the European continent.

In England, another branch of philosophy began to take root. Bertrand Russell was one of the exponents of a philosophy called "linguistic analysis." The loss of faith in the positive view of man caused those in Britain and later in the United States to move toward simply defining words. They thought that by understanding the words used in the English language, communication might become a means toward bringing progress.

The secular existentialist's view is that of existing for the moment. Universality and objectivity gave way to the subjective. In the '60s, the United States was faced with a similar revolution in its society. Although skepticism was mainly located within the major intellectual centers of the country, it was growing in strength. The war in Vietnam was the social shock which gave rise to the disorder which skepticism produces. At that time, patriotism, faith in the Supreme God, and even the most basic elements of the American social framework were attacked.

Although America overcame the most insidious aspects of skepticism, the basic tenets are still at work within its art and music. The social and intellectual implications have been seen in the films and books which have been exported throughout the world. Movies which now portray antiheroes as the main characters, television programs which preach that immorality and sexual promiscuity are acceptable, and books which proclaim the total freedom of the individual at the expense of society's well-being are quickly affecting the rest of the world.

The prosperity of the past decades has only provided more leisure for the practices which we Christians abhor. The illicit use of drugs, even by public and business leaders, crime, pornography as art, and homosexuality are only the symptoms and not the cause of the problems which the local church must face in the future.

The basic problem is skepticism, which attacks the universality and objectivity of truth. What can we do to prepare ourselves to meet the needs of this lost generation?

We are not all philosophers or theologians. But we are all called by Christ to love. We must, therefore, follow three basic principles:

1. Understand the problem.
2. Understand the causes of the problem.
3. Produce the truth in practice.

In so many ways our job of preaching has been made easier. We don't have to meet the misplaced faith man used to have in science and technology to meet the human needs of our society. We also are not facing the great faith man has had in his own inherent goodness (that he does not need to be saved from anything). Therefore, in the present and even more in the future we are going to be able to speak to hearts which are open to the gospel. The attack on truth has brought about a void which can only be filled by Jesus Christ, who is the Truth.

Understanding the Problem. As I have previously stated, the problem is not the disorder in art, music and society in increasing forms. The problem is more complex. It is an increasingly growing dismissal of truth in its universal and objective form. The fact that their argument is irrational does not seem to bother the skeptics, since they have little desire to be rational.

Understanding the cause of the problem. Skepticism has not been arrived at rationally. It was basically an emotional reaction to man's depravity. This is not a new fact to the biblical Christian. The Bible has always taught that unregenerated man was basically sinful and it was only the grace of God that causes man to be moral and upright. Jesus took man's sin to the cross. By trusting in his sacrifice, which satisfies God's justice, man is saved from sin.

The future, then, is ours. Only the evangelical Christian has a universal and objective framework for reality. We have the Creator, the Father. We have the source of understanding, the Holy Spirit. We have the example, the Lord Jesus Christ. And, we have the obvious group which has brought the truth in daily operation, the church.

By catching a vision of unlimited growth as well as by organizing in a way which can effectively handle that growth, the church can fill the void which has been created by the skeptics. Yet, the church must not just rely on its ability to proclaim the reality of the truth in a clear and rational way. She must also proclaim the truth in the power of the Holy Spirit.

4. Restoration of Power

"But ye shall receive power" (Acts 1:8). The difference between preaching the gospel now and the gospel's proclamation in the early church is the question of power. Although we use more powerful means of communication, our message seems to be less potent. The difference is the Holy Spirit. This is not just a statement of individual fact, it is rather a corporate observation.

To understand the problem, we must study the promise. In Acts 1:8, which I have just quoted, there are two principles presented.

1. The promise is corporate in nature. "Ye" is the plural form. The promise of power is given to the disciples as a group. The church has certain promises which can be claimed as a group. Although we can see power being manifested in individual pastors or evangelists, the church as a whole is presently not manifesting the same power that the early church displayed.

The challenge to the church will be increased by the forces of Satan inherent in secularism, skepticism, communism, and materialism. In answer, the church must, and I believe, will, move in a new corporate power.

2. The promise is certain. Jesus did not say, "Ye *may* receive power." No, the promise is positive. "Ye *shall* receive power." Christ's certainty in the power manifested by the church after Pentecost was not in the disciple's ability, courage or will. Rather it was in the ability of the Holy Spirit.

The Holy Spirit was able to take men and women who were not humanly gifted and cause divine gifts to flow through them. He was able to take an apostle like Peter who had denied Christ three times in one night, and cause him to stand courageously before a potentially hostile crowd of Jews from all over the Roman Empire. Courageously Peter proclaimed the gospel of Jesus Christ in great clarity and power.

Christ could be certain because of the Holy Spirit. The same Holy Spirit must be relied upon in the end of this age to make shepherds out of what we now call pastors, evangelists out of prophetic proclaimers, and strong witnesses out of disinterested laity.

5. Power in Action

We need power to witness. Christ's promise in Acts 1:8, RSV, was definite: "Ye shall be my witnesses." The "dunamos" of God not only suggests strength of force but also dynamics of purpose. The power which Christ promised would make the disciples witnesses, "martas" translated from the Greek into English. Witness carries three basic aspects:

a. Martyr is the English word derived from "Martas." Therefore, the word witness signifies sacrifice. The Holy Spirit gives power to the church in order for her to proclaim the good news of Jesus Christ—even if it means great sacrifice. In fact, in the areas of the world where the church is sacrificing the most, her witness is most powerful.

b. In classical Greek, the word signified a person who was a witness at a trial. The most credible witnesses were those who had first-hand knowledge of a particular event. If a court witness is merely repeating what he has heard someone else say, his testimony is deemed hearsay. It is considered inadmissible and is stricken from the court records.

The Holy Spirit gives power to the church to experience the splendor and glory of Christ first-hand. Then she can proclaim the Good News of Christ's Lordship as an eyewitness. This witness is both sure and credible.

c. The witness was to be specific: "*My* witnesses." The Holy Spirit gave the church power to witness the Good News of Jesus Christ. She was not to preach any other message. Although the gospel has social, political, and economic implications, the basic message of the church must remain: "Jesus Christ and Him crucified."

A perfect example of this is found in the life of Paul. Chapters 17 and 18 of Acts reveal a "tale of two cities," Athens and Corinth. Athens was the intellectual center of the Western world. Corinth was a powerful industrial center.

In Athens, Paul traveling alone, proclaimed the gospel to the city by using his intellectual power. In Corinth, Paul—accompanied by Timothy, Silas, Aquila and Priscilla—proclaimed the gospel not only in a rational way, but he exhibited the power of the Holy Spirit. In Athens, Paul's stay was short. In Corinth, he stayed six months.

In Athens we read of no great miracles taking place. In Corinth the situation was different. "My message and my preaching were not in a persuasive, learned oratory, but rather in evidence of the Spirit and power" (1 Cor. 2:4, MLB). In Athens, the biblical record does not indicate that the church was established. In Corinth, a strong and gifted church was established although it was divided into factions. If the church is to experience dynamic growth, she must recognize, as one body, the promise of Christ. His desire is for the church to proclaim the message in power so that a skeptical world will have a clear witness.

The whole world may not respond in faith; yet, the whole world must have a clear witness before the end of this age.

6. Restoration of Unity

John 17:24 has been preached, written about and prayed over for many years. Yet, the great goal of Christian unity still evades us. Historically, the greatest hindrance that Christianity has had to overcome in the nonevangelized parts of the world is the many opposing voices which proclaim it.

Before we can overcome the forces that divide us, we should understand who we are in Christ. Paul reveals twenty things the church is in Christ in his Letter to the Ephesians. What follows is a verse-by-verse commentary on selected scriptures from Ephesians.

1. *Chosen* (Eph. 1:4). We are not Christians because we chose Christ, but rather because Christ chose us.

2. *Holy* (Eph. 1:4). We are meant to be a holy people, which means we are set aside into divine service.

3. *Blameless* (Eph. 1:4). Because of the cross, we are free of all blame before God's presence.

4. *Predestined* (Eph. 1:5). We have been predetermined to be conformed in Christ's image.

5. *Favored* (Eph. 1:6). Our union with Christ has brought us into divine favor.

6. *Christ's Heritage* (Eph. 1:11). We are the inheritance Christ received after dying and being raised from the dead.

7. *Foreordained* (Eph. 1:4). God willed that we should belong to Christ even before the physical world was founded.

8. *Praise* (Eph. 1:12). We are meant to be a praise that brings the Father glory.

9. *Sealed* (Eph. 1:13). We have been securely sealed by the Holy Spirit.

10. *God's Property* (Eph. 1:14). We are no longer our own, but we have been bought and paid for at great expense.

11. *Seated* (Eph. 1:20). We are seated on Christ's throne high above all authority in the present and future ages.

12. *His Body* (Eph. 1:23). We make up Christ's physical presence in this world.

13. *His Completeness* (Eph. 1:23). He is only as complete in this world as we are complete as His church.

14. *Alive* (Eph. 2:5). We have been made capable of spiritual perceptibility.

15. *His Handiwork* (Greek, "poema"—Eph. 2:10). We are His creative masterpiece to bring glory to the Great Master.

16. *Fellow Citizens* (Eph. 2:19). We are now fellow citizens with the Old Testament saints of God's nation. We have full rights and privileges.

17. *Members of God's Household* (Eph. 2:19). We are included among God's closest relatives. We are accepted as family.

18. *His Temple* (Eph. 2:21). We are a part of His divine dwelling place.

19. *Joint Heirs* (Eph. 3:6). We are joint heirs with Christ. Therefore, we inherit exactly what Christ inherited.

20. *We Are His Army* (Eph. 6:11–17). We have been given the defensive and offensive weaponry whereby we can combat Satan successfully.

I have stated these twenty positions we enjoy in Christ because we must reassess what we are in order for us to see what we are not. By looking briefly at what we are called in Ephesians, we can notice one glaring similarity: *Not one of the twenty conditions was reached by our efforts.* All of the twenty were given to us by God as a result of the work of Christ.

We are not able to become what God has already made us by his grace. Consequently, it becomes evident that we in our own strength cannot become anything, apart from the grace of God. This is extremely important as we view the subject of unity.

One pervading principle which has guided my ministry for twenty-five years has been, "Find the river of the will of God. Swim into the middle of it and allow the strength of his will to float you in the direction of his divine purpose." I believe this is what the writer of the Letter to the Hebrews means when he tells us to rest. Rest is not passive but active. Yet, it is not our activity or effort. It is the effort of the will of God, which accomplishes lasting results, working within us.

7. The Holy Spirit's Unity

"Making every effort to preserve the unity of the Spirit in the bond of peace" (Eph. 4:3, MLB). The problem with the union which many churches have been trying to accomplish is that their efforts, although noble, are human.

The New Testament church was not divided in rigidly constructed denominations. But the same forces which caused denominational schisms were at work all the same.

There were those who followed Paul, others followed Apollos. Some favored Peter's adherence to Jewish piety, others practiced Timothy's liberty.

The difference was that the early church had a way of dealing with conflicts and doctrinal differences. The councils may not have succeeded in changing the natural proclivities which the early saints had, but they were able to maintain unity through a spirit of communication and fellowship.

We are commanded to guard the unity of the body of Christ. There are three aspects of Ephesians 4:3 which we need to explore in this section.

#1. The unity we are commanded to guard is the unity brought about by the Holy Spirit. The Holy Spirit is the spirit of harmony and not of strife. He nudges all who are sincerely in communication with him toward unity. Unity is an attitude or frame of mind. It does not mean that we will always be in constant communication with every other part of the church, but it does mean that we will be in an attitude of cooperation.

#2. We are to guard or preserve unity. The original word, translated "preserve," has its root meaning in the actions of a sentry. Our attitude must be sentient. We have to be aware, awake, cognizant, and alert. A sentry cannot fall asleep on duty. Paul says we have to guard unity because that is the one thing Satan can usually attack successfully. By destroying our unity, Satan does not have to fear our power.

#3. The maintainer of unity is peace. Tranquillity is one of the most difficult attitudes we are called to maintain. The cares of this world can so easily destroy our peace. Once our peace is disturbed, we are no longer vigilant in keeping the unity of the Holy Spirit. So, it is extremely important to keep our hearts at peace.

8. The Unity of the Faith

The body of Christ will be finally considered mature when the church comes into the unity of the faith. "So He has given some to be apostles and others to be prophets; some to be evangelists and others to be pastors and teachers, to equip the saints for the task of ministering toward the building up of the body of Christ. Until we all may arrive at the unity of the faith and that understanding of the Son of God that brings completeness of personality, tending towards the measure of the stature of the fullness of Christ" (Eph. 4:11–13, MLB).

As I have stated before, the purpose of the ministry is to equip the laity. Yet the job of training the laity will only be completed when we as the church universal enter into a more complete understanding of Christ.

This high and supreme goal will be accomplished as we enter into the unity of the faith.

The first believers found themselves in one place and with one accord when the church was originally conceived by the Holy Spirit. As infants they were idealistic, yet naive.

At the end of the twentieth century we face the same opportunity with the same Holy Spirit who initiated the church. He is working to complete her. We have two thousand years of history to study and understand. We have no excuse if we repeat the mistakes of the past.

Corporate unity will lead to renewed power of message and ministry. Renewed power will lead to unlimited understanding. And this new understanding will bring us into the corporate maturity God is awaiting. The future is not going to be easy. But it is possible for every local expression of Christ to grow both spiritually and numerically.

The restoration process is presently at work. The restoration is not of human origin but demands human preservation. The church growth movement is an integral part of the restoration process. For as we can notice, the challenges of the future must be met on a church-by-church basis. Meaningful Christian growth is accomplished individually in each community empowered by God's Holy Spirit.

Conclusion

In this book, I have tried to create a guide to church growth, based on my twenty-six years of ministry. I have prayed literally hundreds of hours over the material that I have enclosed in this book. I pray that you have been blessed by it.

Now that you have completed your reading of the book, please pray that the Holy Spirit gives you the grace and the power to put into practice the things that you have learned. If you don't use what I have said then your reading has been of little value.

To whom much is given, much is required. Now that you have read and understood what I have said, you are held responsible by God. If you have any questions, you can write me at my New York Office: Church Growth International, Post Office Box 3434, New York, N.Y. 10163.